A FLASH in the Pan

A FLASH in the Pan

Shirley Gill and Liz Trigg

LORENZ BOOKS
NEW YORK • LONDON • SYDNEY • BATH

This edition published in the UK in 1997 by Lorenz Books

This edition published in the USA by Lorenz Books,
27 West 20th Street,
New York, NY 10011

LORENZ BOOKS are available for bulk purchase for sales promotion and for premium use.
For details write or call the manager of special sales: Lorenz Books, 27 West 20th Street,
New York, NY (212) 807-6739.

Lorenz Books is an imprint of
Anness Publishing Limited

ISBN 1 85967 480 1

Publisher: Joanna Lorenz
Senior Cookery Editor: Linda Fraser
Designers: Adrian Morris and Peter Laws
Photographers: Amanda Heywood and Michelle Garrett
Home Economists: Nicola Fowler and Liz Trigg

Printed and bound in Hong Kong

1 3 5 7 9 10 8 6 4 2

CONTENTS

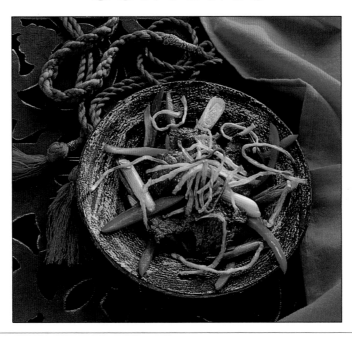

Introduction	6
Techniques	18
SNACKS AND APPETIZERS	26
FISH AND SEAFOOD DISHES	50
MEAT AND POULTRY DISHES	80
VEGETABLE AND VEGETARIAN DISHES	124
RICE AND NOODLE DISHES	158
DESSERTS	184
Index	190

INTRODUCTION

Stir-frying is an ancient cooking technique that originated in the Far East, but its popularity has spread throughout the world. It is an ideal technique for the modern cook: dishes can be stir-fried in a matter of minutes, using very little oil, which means the ingredients lose little of their nutritional value, and are relatively low in fat.

Many of the recipes in this book are Oriental favorites, originating from all over the Far East, but traditional Western dishes have been adapted to take advantage of this quick technique – you'll find recipes for Beef Sukiyaki and Duck and Ginger Chop Suey, Chicken Liver Stir-fry and stir-fried Turkey with Sage. Don't be afraid to try the recipes if you haven't got a wok – a large frying pan with a heavy base will work just as well, although you may find in some cases it is necessary to cook the ingredients in smaller batches.

Once you begin, you'll be amazed at the versatility of the technique, and may find you can adapt some of your own favorites. Whether you want a spicy starter or a sizzling dessert, consider stir-frying for a quick, healthy and delicious dish.

Equipment

You will find most of the cooking equipment you have around the kitchen will produce good results. As mentioned previously, it isn't even essential to use a wok. However, if you would like to invest in some good kitchen equipment, or wish to use the authentic tools of the trade, the following may be of interest:

Bamboo skewers
These are widely used for barbecues and grilled foods. They are discarded after use.

Chopping board
A good quality chopping board with a thick surface will last for years.

Chopping knife
If you are not comfortable using a cleaver, a large, heavy chopping knife can be used.

Citrus zester
This tool is designed to remove the zest while leaving the bitter white pith. It can also be used for shaving fresh coconut.

Cleaver
The weight of the cleaver makes it ideal for chopping all kinds of ingredients. Keep this as sharp as possible.

Cooking chopsticks
These are extra-long, and allow you to stir ingredients in the wok, while keeping a safe distance.

Draining wire
This is designed to sit on the side of the wok, and is used mainly for deep-frying.

Food processor
This is a quick alternative to the pestle and mortar.

Ladle
A long-handled ladle is very useful for spooning out soup, stock or sauces.

Pestle and mortar
This is useful for grinding small amounts of spices.

Rice paddle
This is used to fluff up rice after cooking.

Saucepan
A good saucepan with a tight-fitting lid is essential for cooking rice properly. It may also be used for stir-frying.

Sharpening stone
A traditional tool for sharpening knives and cleavers, available from hardware stores.

Stainless steel skimmer
This can be used when strong flavors are likely to affect bare metal cooking implements.

Wire skimmer
This is used to remove cooked food from boiling water or hot fat. It should not be used with fish-based liquids as the strong flavor is likely to affect the metal.

Wok
The shape of the wok allows ingredients to be cooked in a minimum of fat, thus retaining freshness and flavor. There are several varieties available including the carbon steel round-bottomed wok or Pau wok. This wok is best suited to a gas burner, where you will be able to control the amount of heat needed more easily. The carbon steel flat-bottomed wok is best for use on electric or gas burners, as it will create a better distribution of heat. A small round-bottomed wok enables you to prepare small quantities quickly, as it takes less time to heat up.

wok

*cooking
chopsticks*

*stainless
steel skimmers*

lad...

food processor

bamboo skewers

saucepan

chopping board

chopping
knife

draining
wire

sharpening
stone

citrus
zester

cleavers

pestle and
mortar

rice paddle

wire skimmer

Fresh Produce

Almost any ingredient can be stir-fried, and, as the freshness and flavor of the produce will not be affected by cooking, it is important to choose the freshest, best quality ingredients you can.

Baby corn
These may be stir-fried whole or chopped.

Bean sprouts
These impart a lovely texture to vegetable and meat dishes. Do not keep for longer than a few days or they will wilt.

Coconut
Fresh coconut is infinitely better tasting than any other coconut product available. When selecting a coconut, choose one with plenty of milk inside.

Cress
This is usually added at the last moment, or as a garnish.

Cucumber
Cucumber can be chopped and sliced finely and stir-fried, or used in relishes.

Fennel
Slice and stir-fry to impart an aniseed flavor.

Garlic
Crush or chop finely.

Jicama
This has a very subtle flavor.

Leeks
Slice into very thin rings before stir-frying.

Lemons
Use the grated rind and juice in stir-fries and marinades, and lemon slices as a garnish.

Limes
Use the grated rind and juice in stir-fries and marinades, and lime slices as a garnish.

Lychees
Peel to use, remove the pit, and halve or slice.

Mango
Ripe mango should have a slightly soft flesh. Peel and remove the stone before use.

Napa cabbage
The crispy leaves are ideal for stir-frying. Shred or chop finely before using.

Onions
Every variety of onion makes a tasty addition to stir-fries.

Oyster mushrooms
Use as ordinary mushrooms, wiping clean with a damp cloth or paper towel.

Patty pan squash
These small squash taste similar to yellow squash.

Peppers
Deseed and chop into strips before stir-frying.

Radishes
Slice finely, or use tiny baby radishes as a garnish.

Scallions
Chop finely before using, or cut into julienne strips.

Shiitake mushrooms
These tasty, firm-textured mushrooms may be treated as ordinary mushrooms. Only use half the amount if using the dried variety. Soak in boiling water for 20 minutes, and save the soaking water for a sauce.

Spinach
Remove the stalks before using and wash thoroughly in several changes of cold water to remove any grit.

Counter-clockwise from top left: *red peppers, coconuts, lychees, shiitake mushrooms, spinach, onions, bean sprouts, cress, Napa cabbage, jicama, radishes, baby corn, scallions, leeks, oyster and shiitake mushrooms, yellow pepper, fennel, celery.* In center basket, from top left: *patty pan squash. mango, limes, garlic, lemons.*

Herbs and Spices

The following can be used to enhance fresh ingredients. Whenever possible, use fresh herbs for the best flavor. If using dried herbs you will need smaller amounts as the flavor is less subtle. Some of the flavorings used in this book include the following:

Chilies
Generally, the smallest chilies are the hottest. Removing the seeds will reduce the heat. Chop finely, and stir-fry with oil. Always work in a well-ventilated area and do not allow chilies to come into contact with your skin or eyes.

Chili powder
Many varieties of dried chili powder are now available, each varying in strength.

Chinese chives
These have a mild flavor similar to a Spanish onion. They should be cooked very lightly and are wonderful served raw as a garnish.

Coriander leaves
Fresh coriander imparts a unique, refreshing taste and aroma. Bunches of fresh leaves can be kept for up to 5 days in a jar of water.

Coriander seeds
Whole seeds can be dry-fried (without oil) with other ingredients and are also available ground.

Cumin
Cumin is generally dry-fried and combines well with coriander seeds. It is widely used in beef dishes.

Galingale
This is sometimes known as Lengkuas. This root has a mingled flavor of pine and citrus. It may be peeled and treated in the same way as ginger root.

Ginger root
Peel off the skin of the fresh root and use sliced, chopped or grated. Always buy the roots with the smoothest skin as it is the freshest. The flesh should be a creamy color, and not too yellow.

Lemon grass
This aromatic herb has a thin tapering stem and a citrusy, verbena flavor. To use, thinly slice the bulb end of the root.

Lime leaves
These are often called kaffir lime leaves. They are excellent in marinades, and often need to be bruised to release the flavor.

Paprika
Paprika is made from a variety of sweet red pepper. It is mild in flavor, and adds color. Add to stir-fries or sprinkle on finished dishes.

Parsley
Parsley, both curly and flat-leaf, is an ideal and attractive garnish. Flat-leaf parsley has a stronger flavor than the curly variety.

Rosemary
This is usually added to lamb and pork dishes. It has a strong flavor.

Star anise
This spice has a pungent, aniseed-like taste. It can either be ground, or used whole in marinades.

Turmeric
Turmeric is used for its attractive yellow coloring. It has a slightly musty taste and aroma.

Right: *Flavor enhancers for stir-fries might include herbs such as parsley, rosemary, or coriander, or spices such as chili powder, cumin, paprika, turmeric, ginger or star anise. Lemon grass, lime leaves, galingale or fresh chilies will add a distinctly eastern flavor.*

Flavoring Ingredients

The following ingredients can be used to create authentic tasting Eastern stir-fries. They can be purchased in most large supermarkets or Oriental food stores.

Creamed coconut
This is available in a solid block form from Oriental food stores and large supermarkets and is ideal for giving an intense coconut flavor. Simply add water to make a thick coconut paste. The paste may be thinned with more water until the correct consistency and flavor is acquired.

Extra-virgin olive oil
This is the highest grade olive oil and has a very intense flavor. Do not use this oil for cooking, but drizzle it over the finished dish before serving.

Grapeseed oil
A lightly flavored oil, good for stir-frying delicately flavored foods.

Hoisin sauce
This is often called barbecue sauce, and is a spicy/smoky condiment with a distinctive smoky flavor.

Olive oil
The characteristic flavor of olive oil is not suitable for Oriental stir-fries. Use it instead when you want to impart a distinctive Mediterranean flavor.

Oyster sauce
Made from oyster extract, this specialty sauce is used in many fish dishes, soups and sauces.

Peanut butter
This can be used in Indonesian satay dishes. It makes a good sauce when heated. Use varieties of peanut butter with no added sugar for the best flavor.

Red chili sauce
A sweet, hot sauce that is often used to flavor home-made sauces, or used on its own as a dip.

Red wine vinegar
Use this vinegar for sauces, dressings and marinades for a robust flavor.

Sake (rice wine)
Sake is used mainly in Japanese stir-fries. The best grades are used for drinking, and the lower grades for sauces and marinades, and also for dressings.

Sesame oil
This is used more as a flavoring than for cooking. It is very intensely flavored, so only a few drops will be needed at a time.

Sherry vinegar
Use for sauces and marinades for a strong flavor.

Soy sauce
Dark soy sauce is sweet and thick, and the best variety is made from naturally fermented soy. Light soy sauce is a less intense version of the classic dark soy sauce.

Sugar
Both superfine sugar and soft brown sugar are used in marinades and sauces.

Sunflower oil
A good all-purpose cooking oil with a mild flavor.

Teriyaki sauce
Use in barbecued and stir-fried dishes, and as a marinade for meat or fish.

White wine vinegar
Use for sauces, marinades and dressings.

sesame oil

olive oil

creamed coconut

red chili sauce

brown sugar

white wine vinegar

sake (rice wine)

extra-virgin olive oil

sherry vinegar

grapeseed oil

sunflower oil

red wine
vinegar

peanut
butter

teriyaki sauce

light
soy
sauce

sugar

oyster sauce

dark soy sauce

hoisin sauce

Vegetables and Pantry Ingredients

Most of the vegetables used in this book will be familiar to you, but descriptions of some of the more exotic ones are given below for those who are more adventurous. Remember always to buy the best and freshest vegetables and cook them for only a short time so that they retain their crispness, color and nutrients.

Bak Choy
An attractive vegetable with a long, smooth, milky-white stem and large, dark green leaves.

Bamboo Shoots
These mild-flavored tender shoots of the young bamboo are available fresh in Asian stores, or sliced and halved in cans. Clean thoroughly before use.

Beansprouts
These shoots of the mung bean are usually available from supermarkets. They add a crisp texture to stir-fries.

Canned Corn
Baby corn cobs have a crunchy texture and a mild, sweet flavor and are an attractive ingredient. They are widely available from supermarkets, mostly in canned or bottled form, or frozen.

Chinese Cabbage
Sometimes known as Napa cabbage. It looks like a large, tightly packed Romaine lettuce with firm, pale green, crinkled leaves. It has a delicious crunchy texture.

Chinese Long Beans
These are long thin beans similar to green beans but three or four times longer. Cut into smaller lengths and use just like ordinary green beans.

Chinese Pancakes
These are flour-and-water pancakes with no seasonings or spices added. They are available fresh or frozen; if using frozen pancakes, thaw them thoroughly before steaming them.

Gram Flour
Gram flour is made from ground chickpeas and has a unique flavor. It is well worth seeking out in Indian food stores or health-food stores, but if you prefer you can use plain wholewheat flour instead, adding extra water.

Mushrooms
Both fresh and dried mushrooms can be used in wok cookery to add texture and flavor to a dish. Dried mushrooms need to be soaked in warm water for 20–30 minutes before use. The soaking liquor, once it has been strained, can be used as a stock. Although dried mushrooms are expensive per package, only a few are needed per recipe and they can be stored indefinitely.

Noodles
A wide variety of fresh and dried noodles is available. These can be interchanged in most recipes. Some types of noodles may require quick cooking, while others need soaking in boiling water. They can be made from wheat, rice, ground beans or buckwheat. Follow the cooking instructions on the package.

Rice
For the purposes of this book long-grain white rice is used, varying from Thai jasmine to Indian basmati. Long-grain rices such as patna and basmati tend to be drier and their grains remain separate when cooked; Thai jasmine rice, though delicious, is soft, light and stickier. Directions for cooking rice are in individual recipes.

Scallions
This slender spring onion is the immature bulb of the yellow onion. When recipes refer to the "white" part this is the firm, mainly white section which makes up most of the onion; "green" is the leaves.

Shallots
Shallots are small mild-flavored members of the onion family with copper-red skins. They can be used in the same way as onions or ground into Thai curry pastes or fried into crisp flakes to be used as a garnish.

Snow Peas
These tender green peapods, containing flat, barely formed peas, are highly valued for their crisp texture and sweet flavor.

Spring Roll Wrappers
Paper-thin wrappers made from wheat flour or rice flour and water. They are available from most Asian grocers. Wheat flour wrappers are sold frozen and need to be thawed and carefully separated before use. Rice wrappers are dry and must be gently soaked before use.

Tofu
Tofu is also known as bean curd. Blocks of firm tofu are used in the recipes in this book as it is more suitable for stir-frying and deep-frying. Although rather bland in flavor, it readily absorbs the flavors of other ingredients. It can be stored in the fridge for several days covered with water.

Water Chestnuts
A walnut-sized bulb of an Asian water plant that resembles a chestnut with its outer brown layer. Once peeled, the flesh is crisp and sweet. They are sold fresh by some Asian grocers, but are more readily available canned, whole or sliced.

Wonton Wrappers
Paper-thin squares of yellow-colored dough, these are sold in most Asian food stores.

Top shelf, left to right: *egg noodles, wonton wrappers, water chestnuts, cellophane noodles, gram flour, spring roll wrappers*

Middle shelf, left to right: *dried Chinese mushrooms, bok choy, tofu, egg noodles, Chinese pancakes*

Bottom, left to right: *rice, (in basket) snow peas, corn, shallots, shiitake mushrooms, bamboo shoots, beansprouts, Chinese cabbage, scallions, Chinese long beans*

At front: *wood ears (mushrooms)*

Preparing Ingredients

While stir-frying is quick and easy, it is essential to know how to prepare ingredients for cooking in order to be successful. Asian cooks always use a cleaver for these tasks, but a sharp heavy knife can be used instead. For the ingredients to cook as quickly as possible and properly absorb the taste of the oil and flavorings despite the short cooking time, they should be cut into small uniform pieces and as many cut surfaces as possible should be exposed to the heat. Another important reason for careful cutting is to enhance the visual appeal of a dish. This is why most Asian cuisines are so specific about cutting techniques, particularly vegetables.

VEGETABLES

Some vegetables such as broccoli and cauliflower are cut according to their natural shape into florets; others are sliced, diagonally sliced, shredded, diced or roll cut depending on the dish.

MEAT

Meat for stir-frying and sometimes steaming is cut into thin slices, matchstick strips or cubes. This way it can be quickly stir-fried or steamed without losing any of its tenderness.

1 Diagonal cutting is a technique used for cutting vegetables such as carrots, asparagus or scallions. It allows more of the surface of the vegetable to be exposed for quicker cooking. Simply angle the cleaver or knife at a slant and cut.

2 Roll cutting is like diagonal cutting but is used for larger vegetables such as zucchini, eggplant or large carrots. Start by making one diagonal slice at one end of the vegetable, then turn it 180° and make the next diagonal cut. Continue until you have cut the entire vegetable into even-size chunks.

1 Beef is always cut across the grain, otherwise it would become tough; pork, lamb and chicken can be cut either along or across the grain.

2 Placing the meat in the freezer for about 1 hour beforehand makes it easier to cut paper-thin slices.

CHOPPING HERBS

1 Strip the leaves from the stalks and pile them on a chopping board.

2 Using a cleaver or chef's knife, cut the herbs into small pieces, moving the blade back and forth until the herbs are as coarse or fine as you wish.

PEELING AND CHOPPING LEMONGRASS

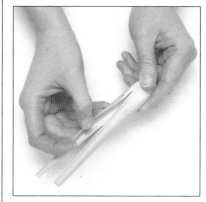

1 Cut off and discard the dry leafy tops, leaving about 6 in of stalk. Peel away any tough outer layers from the lemongrass.

2 Lay the lemongrass on a board. Set a cleaver or chef's knife on top and strike it firmly with your fist – this helps to extract maximum flavor. Cut across the lemongrass to make thin slices, then continue chopping until fine.

PREPARING BEANSPROUTS

1 Pick over the beansprouts, discarding any that are discolored, broken or wilted.

2 Rinse the beansprouts under cold running water and drain well.

PREPARING KAFFIR LIME LEAVES

1 Using a small sharp knife, remove the center vein.

2 Cut the leaves crosswise into very fine strips.

PEELING AND CHOPPING GARLIC

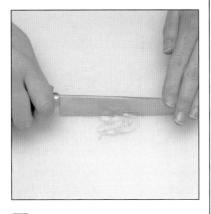

1 Lay the unpeeled garlic clove on a board. Set the flat side of a cleaver or chef's knife on top and strike it firmly with your fist.

2 Peel off and discard the skin. Finely chop the garlic, using the cleaver, moving the blade back and forth.

CUTTING AND SHREDDING GARLIC AND GINGER

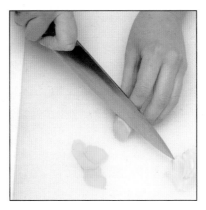

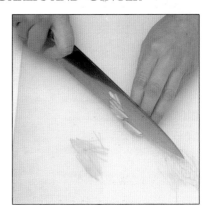

1 Peel the skin from the ginger or garlic clove. Using a cleaver or chef's knife, cut into thin slices.

2 To cut into shreds, arrange the slices one on top of another and cut lengthwise into fine strips.

PEELING AND CHOPPING GINGER

1 Using a small sharp knife, peel the skin from the ginger.

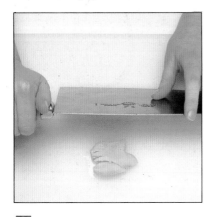

2 Place the ginger on a board. Set the flat side of a cleaver or chef's knife on top and strike it firmly with your fist – this will soften its fibrous texture.

3 Chop the ginger as coarsely or finely as you wish, moving the blade backwards and forwards.

REMOVING SEEDS FROM CHILIES

1 Wearing rubber gloves, remove the stalks from chilies.

2 Cut in half lengthwise.

3 Using a small sharp knife, scrape out the seeds and fleshy white ribs from each half.

Garnishes

Many Asian dishes rely on garnishes to add a colorful finishing decorative touch. The garnishes can be simple, such as chopped cilantro, fresh herb sprigs, or finely shredded scallions or chili, or more elaborate, such as cucumber fans, scallion brushes and chili flowers.

CHILI FLOWER

1 Make several lengthwise cuts through a chili from below the stalk to the tip. Remove and discard any seeds.

2 Soak the chili in iced water until the ends curl to form a "flower". Pat dry with paper towels before use.

CUCUMBER FAN

1 Cut a slice of cucumber lengthwise, about 3 in long, avoiding the seeds. Remove any skin and cut into strips to within ½ in from the end. Remove alternate strips.

2 Carefully bend the strips towards the uncut end, tucking them in so that they stay securely in place. Allow to soak in iced water until required and pat dry before use.

SCALLION BRUSH

1 Trim the green part of a scallion and remove the base of the bulb – you should then be left with a piece about 3 in long. Then make a lengthwise cut approximately 1 in long at one end of the scallion.

2 Roll the scallion through 90° and cut again. Repeat this process at the other end. Place in iced water until the shreds open out and curl. Pat dry with paper towels before use.

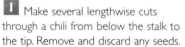

Spice Mixtures and Stocks

Use these spice mixtures to add heat and flavor to Thai curries, fish cakes and kadhai dishes. They are quick and easy to make, but you can buy them ready-made from larger supermarkets.

THAI RED CURRY PASTE

INGREDIENTS
4 fresh red chilies
1-in piece fresh ginger
4 shallots
4–6 garlic cloves
4 lemongrass stalks
4 tsp coriander seeds
2 tsp cumin seeds
2 tsp hot paprika
¼ tsp ground turmeric
½ tsp salt
grated rind and juice of 2 limes
1 tbsp vegetable oil

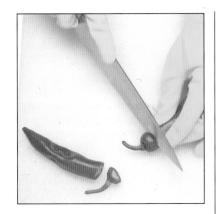

1 Peel and chop the ginger, shallots and garlic. Peel and finely chop the lemongrass. Wearing rubber gloves, remove the stalks from the chilies, then cut them in half lengthwise. Scrape out the seeds and fleshy white ribs, then coarsely chop the flesh.

THAI GREEN CURRY PASTE

INGREDIENTS
6 scallions
4 cilantro stems, washed
4 kaffir lime leaves
6–8 fresh green chilies
4 garlic cloves, chopped
1-in piece fresh ginger, chopped
1 lemongrass stalk, chopped
3 tbsp chopped fresh cilantro
3 tbsp chopped fresh basil
1 tbsp vegetable oil

2 Heat a small frying pan over medium heat, then add the coriander and cumin seeds. Toss them in the pan until the spices turn a shade darker and emit a roasted aroma. Allow to cool.

3 Place all the ingredients in a blender or food processor and process to form a smooth paste. Store in a screw-top jar for up to 1 month in the fridge and use as required.

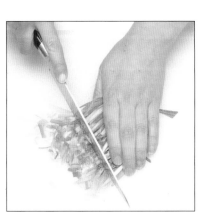

1 Chop the scallions and cilantro stems. Remove the center vein from the kaffir lime leaves, then cut into fine shreds. Seed and chop the chilies.

2 Put all the ingredients in a blender or food processor and process to form a smooth paste. Store in a screw-top jar for up to 2 weeks in the fridge and use as required.

GARAM MASALA

INGREDIENTS
3-in piece cinnamon stick
2 bay leaves
1 tsp cumin seeds
1 tsp whole cloves
1 tsp black peppercorns
¼ nutmeg, grated

1 Break the cinnamon stick into pieces. Crumble the bay leaves.

2 Heat a small frying pan over medium heat, then add the bay leaves and all the spices except the nutmeg. Dry-roast until the spices turn a shade darker and emit a roasted aroma, stirring or shaking the pan frequently to prevent burning. Allow to cool. Place all the ingredients in a spice mill or electric coffee grinder and grind to a fine powder. Store in a small jar with a tight-fitting lid for up to 2 months.

CHICKEN STOCK

INGREDIENTS
2¼ lb uncooked chicken bones, such as backs, wings etc.
1¼ lb chicken pieces
10 cups water
2 thin slices fresh ginger
2 scallions, white parts only
2 unpeeled garlic cloves
salt, to taste

1 Place all the ingredients except the salt in a large pan and bring to a simmer. Skim off any scum. Simmer for 3–4 hours to extract all the flavor. Season with salt to taste.

2 Strain the stock, pressing the solid ingredients with the back of a ladle or spoon to extract all the liquid. Allow the stock to cool, then chill. Spoon off the fat from the surface. Use as required.

FRESH COCONUT MILK

INGREDIENTS
grated fresh coconut, to fill a measuring jug to the 1⅔ cups mark
1¼ cups hot water

1 First you will need to break open a fresh coconut. To do this, push a skewer into the three holes in the top of the coconut and drain out the liquid. Place the coconut in a plastic bag and hit it hard with a hammer. To remove the outer shell from the coconut pieces, prise the tip of a small sharp knife between it and the coconut flesh. Remove the inner brown skin using a potato peeler. Grate the flesh.

2 Put the measured grated coconut and hot water into a blender or food processor fitted with a metal blade and process for 1 minute. Strain the coconut mixture through a sieve lined with muslin into a bowl, gathering up the corners of the cloth and squeezing out the liquid. The coconut milk is now ready; stir before use.

left to right:
chicken stock
garam masala
fresh coconut milk

General Rules for Stir-frying

Stir-frying takes very little actual cooking time, often no more than a matter of minutes. For this reason it is important that all the ingredients are prepared ahead of time – washed, peeled or grated as required, and cut to approximately the same shape and size, to ensure even cooking.

1 Always heat the wok (or frying pan, if using) for a few minutes before adding the oil or any other ingredients.

2 If adding oil, swirl the oil into the wok and allow it to heat up before adding the next ingredients.

3 When adding the first ingredients, reduce the heat a little. This will ensure they are not overcooked or burned by the time the remaining ingredients have been added to the wok.

4 Once all the ingredients have been added, quickly increase the heat, as this will allow the dish to cook in the least possible time. This allows the ingredients to retain a crisp, fresh texture, and prevents them from becoming soggy or laden with oil.

5 Use a long handled scoop or spatula to turn the ingredients as you stir-fry. This will allow the ingredients to cook evenly and quickly.

6 It may be easier to slice meat for stir-frying if it has been frozen slightly for an hour or so. By the time you have sliced it, the meat will be thawed to cook.

Slicing Onions

Stir-fry onion slices with the main vegetables. Ensure they are all cut to the same size for even cooking.

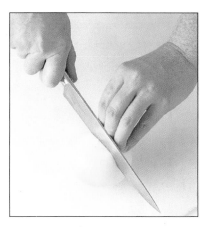

1 Peel the onion. Cut in half with a large knife and set it cut-side down on to a chopping board.

2 Cut out a triangular piece of the core from each half.

3 Cut across each half in vertical slices.

Chopping Onions

Diced onions can be used to flavor oil before stir-frying the main ingredients.

1 Peel the onion. Cut in half with a knife and set it cut-side down on a board. Make lengthwise vertical cuts along the onion, cutting almost through to the root.

2 Make 2 horizontal cuts from the stalk and towards the root, but not through it.

3 Cut the onion crosswise to form small dice.

Mini Spring Rolls

Eat these light crispy parcels with your fingers. If you like slightly spicier food, sprinkle them with a little cayenne pepper before serving.

Makes 20

INGREDIENTS
1 green chili
½ cup vegetable oil
1 small onion, finely chopped
1 clove garlic, crushed
3 oz cooked chicken breast
1 small carrot, cut into fine
    matchsticks
1 scallion, finely sliced
1 small red pepper, seeded and cut
    into fine matchsticks
1 oz bean sprouts
1 tsp sesame oil
4 large sheets filo pastry
1 medium egg white, lightly beaten
long chives, to garnish (optional)
3 tbsp light soy sauce, to serve

scallions

chili

pepper

garlic

bean sprouts

COOK'S TIP
Always keep filo pastry sheets covered with a dry, clean cloth until needed, to prevent them drying out.

1 Carefully remove the seeds from the chili and chop finely, wearing rubber gloves to protect your hands, if necessary.

4 Add the carrot, scallion and red pepper and stir-fry for 2 minutes. Add the bean sprouts, stir in the sesame oil and leave to cool.

2 Heat the wok, then add 2 tbsp of the vegetable oil. When hot, add the onion, garlic and chili. Stir-fry for 1 minute.

5 Cut each sheet of filo into 5 short strips. Place a small amount of filling at one end of each strip, then fold in the long sides and roll up the pastry. Seal and glaze the parcels with the egg white, then chill uncovered for 15 minutes before frying.

3 Slice the chicken thinly, then add to the wok and fry over a high heat, stirring constantly until browned.

6 Wipe out the wok with paper towels, heat it, and add the remaining vegetable oil. When the oil is hot, fry the rolls in batches until crisp and golden brown. Drain on paper towels and serve dipped in light soy sauce.

COOK'S TIP
Be careful to avoid touching your face or eyes when deseeding and chopping chilies because they are very potent and may cause burning and irritation to the skin. Try preparing chilies under running water.

Lettuce-wrapped Garlic Lamb

This tasty first course lamb is stir-fried with garlic, ginger and spices, then served in crisp lettuce leaves with yogurt, a dab of lime pickle and mint leaves – the contrast of hot and spicy and cool and crisp is excellent.

VARIATION
Vegetables, such as cooked diced potatoes or peas, can be added to the ground lamb mixture.

Serves 4

INGREDIENTS
1 lb lamb, shoulder cutlet
½ tsp cayenne pepper
2 tsp ground coriander
1 tsp ground cumin
½ tsp ground turmeric
2 tbsp peanut oil
3–4 garlic cloves, chopped
1 tbsp grated fresh ginger
⅔ cup lamb stock or water
4–6 scallions, sliced
2 tbsp chopped fresh cilantro
15 ml/1 tbsp lemon juice
lettuce leaves, yogurt, lime pickle and mint leaves, to serve

cilantro

stock

garlic

lamb

ginger

peanut oil

scallions

1 Trim the lamb cutlet of any fat and cube into small pieces, then grind in a blender or food processor, taking care not to over-process.

2 In a bowl mix together the cayenne pepper, ground coriander, cumin and turmeric. Add the lamb and rub the spice mixture into the meat. Cover and let marinate for about 1 hour.

3 Heat a wok until hot. Add the oil and swirl it around. When hot, add the garlic and ginger and allow to sizzle for a few seconds.

4 Add the lamb and continue to stir-fry for 2–3 minutes.

5 Pour in the stock and continue to stir-fry until all the stock has been absorbed and the lamb is tender, adding more stock if necessary.

6 Add the scallions, fresh cilantro and lemon juice, then stir-fry for another 30–45 seconds. Serve at once with the lettuce leaves, yogurt, pickle and mint leaves.

Crispy "Seaweed" with Flaked Almonds

This popular appetizer in Chinese restaurants is in fact usually made not with seaweed but spring greens such as collard or chard! It is easy to make at home.

Serves 4-6

INGREDIENTS
1 lb spring greens
peanut oil, for deep-frying
¼ tsp sea salt flakes
1 tsp caster sugar
½ cup flaked almonds,
   toasted

spring greens

almonds

peanut oil

sea salt

sugar

1 Wash the spring greens under cold running water and then pat well with paper towels to dry thoroughly. Remove and discard the thick white stalks from the greens.

COOK'S TIP
It is important to dry the spring greens thoroughly before deep-frying them, otherwise it will be difficult to achieve the desired crispness without destroying their vivid color. ·

2 Lay several leaves on top of one another, roll up tightly and, using a sharp knife, slice as finely as possible into thread-like strips.

3 Half-fill a wok with oil and heat to 350°F. Deep-fry the greens in batches for about 1 minute until they darken and crisp. Remove each batch from the wok as soon as it is ready and drain on paper towels.

4 Transfer the "seaweed" to a serving dish, sprinkle with the salt and sugar, then mix well. Garnish with the toasted flaked almonds sprinkled over.

Sesame Seed Chicken Bites

Best served warm, these crunchy bites are delicious accompanied by a glass of chilled dry white wine.

Makes 20

INGREDIENTS
6 oz raw chicken breast
2 cloves garlic, crushed
1 in piece ginger root, peeled
    and grated
1 medium egg white
1 tsp cornstarch
¼ cup shelled pistachios, roughly
    chopped
4 tbsp sesame seeds
2 tbsp grapeseed oil
salt and freshly ground black pepper

FOR THE SAUCE
¼ cup hoisin sauce
1 tbsp sweet chili sauce

TO GARNISH
ginger root, finely shredded
pistachios, roughly chopped
fresh dill sprigs

sesame seeds

egg

pistachios

garlic

ginger

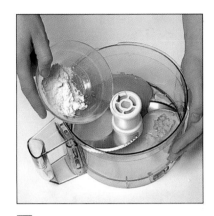

1 Place the chicken, garlic, grated ginger, egg white and cornstarch into the food processor and process them to a smooth paste.

2 Stir in the pistachios and season well with salt and pepper.

3 Roll into 20 balls and coat with sesame seeds. Heat the wok and add the oil. When the oil is hot, stir-fry the chicken bites in batches, turning regularly until golden. Drain on paper towels.

4 Make the sauce by mixing together the hoisin and chili sauces in a bowl. Garnish the bites with shredded ginger, pistachios and dill, then serve hot, with a dish of sauce for dipping.

Mixed Spiced Nuts

These make an excellent accompaniment to drinks. They will store for up to a month in an air-tight container if they are not mixed together.

Serves 4–6

INGREDIENTS
3 oz dried unsweetened
   shredded coconut
5 tbsp peanut oil
½ tsp chili powder
1 tsp ground paprika
1 tsp tomato paste
2 cups unsalted cashews
2 cups whole blanched almonds
4 tbsp superfine sugar
1 tsp ground cumin
½ tsp salt
freshly ground black pepper
cress, to garnish

cashews

paprika

chili powder

cumin

almonds

1 Heat the wok, add the coconut and dry-fry until golden. Leave to cool.

2 Heat the wok and add 3 tbsp of the peanut oil. When the oil is hot, add the chili, paprika and tomato paste. Gently stir-fry the cashews in the spicy mix until well coated. Drain well and season. Leave to cool.

3 Wipe out the wok with paper towels, heat it, then add the remaining oil. When the oil is hot, add the almonds and sprinkle in the sugar. Stir-fry gently until the almonds are golden brown and the sugar is caramelized. Place the cumin and salt in a bowl. Add the almonds, toss well, then leave to cool.

4 Mix the cashews, almonds and coconut together, garnish with cress and serve with drinks.

Thai Fish Cakes

Bursting with the flavors of chilies, lime and lemongrass, these little fish cakes make a wonderful appetizer.

Serves 4

INGREDIENTS
1 lb white fish fillets, such as
  cod or haddock
3 scallions, sliced
2 tbsp chopped fresh cilantro
2 tbsp Thai red curry paste
1 fresh green chili,
  seeded and chopped
2 tsp grated lime rind
1 tbsp lime juice
2 tbsp peanut oil
salt, to taste
crisp lettuce leaves,
  shredded scallions,
  fresh red chili slices,
  cilantro sprigs and
  lime wedges, to serve

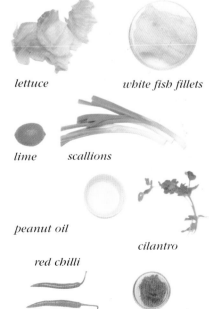

lettuce

white fish fillets

lime

scallions

peanut oil

cilantro

red chilli

green chili   Thai red curry paste

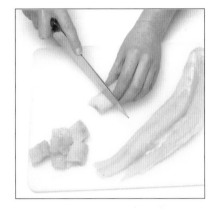

1 Cut the fish into chunks, then place in a blender or food processor.

2 Add the scallions, cilantro, red curry paste, green chili, lime rind and juice to the fish. Season with salt. Process until finely ground.

3 Using lightly floured hands, divide the mixture into 16 pieces and shape each one into a small cake about 1½ in across. Place the fish cakes on a plate, cover with plastic wrap and chill for about 2 hours, until firm. Heat the wok over high heat until hot. Add the oil and swirl it around.

4 Fry the fish cakes, a few at a time, for 6–8 minutes, turning them carefully until evenly browned. Drain each batch on paper towels and keep hot while cooking the remainder. Serve on a bed of crisp lettuce leaves with shredded scallions, red chili slices, cilantro sprigs and lime wedges.

Chinese Spiced Salt Spareribs

Fragrant with spices, this authentic Chinese dish makes a great beginning to an informal meal. Don't forget the finger bowls!

Serves 4

INGREDIENTS
1½–2 lb meaty pork spareribs
1½ tbsp cornstarch
peanut oil, for deep frying
cilantro sprigs, to garnish

FOR THE SPICED SALT
1 tsp Szechuan peppercorns
2 tbsp coarse sea salt
½ tsp Chinese five-
   spice powder

FOR THE MARINADE
2 tbsp light soy sauce
1 tsp caster sugar
1 tbsp Chinese rice wine
ground black pepper

1 Using a heavy sharp cleaver, chop the spareribs into pieces about 2 in long or ask your butcher to do this, then place them in a shallow dish.

2 To make the spiced salt, heat a wok to medium heat. Add the Szechuan peppercorns and salt and dry-fry for about 3 minutes, stirring constantly, until the mixture colors slightly. Remove from the heat and stir in the five-spice powder. Allow to cool.

3 Using a mortar and pestle or an electric coffee grinder, grind the spiced salt to a fine powder.

Chinese rice wine

pork spareribs

Szechuan peppercorns

Chinese five-spice powder

cilantro

light soy sauce

peanut oil

sea salt

4 Sprinkle 1 tsp of the spiced salt over the spareribs and rub in well with your hands. Add the soy sauce, sugar, rice wine or sherry and some freshly ground black pepper, then toss the ribs in the marinade until well coated. Cover and allow to marinate in the fridge for about 2 hours, turning the spareribs occasionally.

COOK'S TIP

Any leftover spiced salt can be kept for several months in a screw-top jar. Use to rub on the flesh of duck, chicken or pork before cooking.

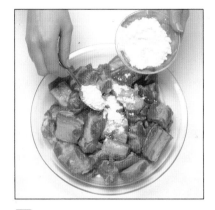

5 Pour off any excess marinade from the spareribs. Sprinkle the pieces with cornstarch and mix well to coat evenly.

6 Half-fill a wok with oil and heat to 350°F. Deep-fry the spareribs in batches for 3 minutes, until pale golden. Remove and set aside. Reheat the oil to the same temperature. Return the spareribs to the oil and deep-fry for a second time for 1–2 minutes, until crisp and thoroughly cooked. Drain on paper towels. Transfer the ribs to a warmed serving platter and sprinkle over 1–1½ tsp spiced salt. Garnish with cilantro sprigs.

Butterfly Shrimp

Use raw shrimp if you can because the flavor will be better, but if you substitute cooked shrimp, cut down the stir-fry cooking time by one third.

Serves 4

INGREDIENTS
1 in piece ginger root
12 oz raw shrimp, thawed
 if frozen
½ cup raw peanuts, roughly
 chopped
3 tbsp vegetable oil
1 clove garlic, crushed
1 red chili, finely chopped
3 tbsp smooth peanut butter
1 tbsp fresh coriander, chopped
fresh coriander sprigs, to garnish

FOR THE DRESSING
⅔ cup natural low-fat yogurt
2 in piece cucumber, diced
salt and freshly ground black pepper

diced cucumber

peanuts

shrimp

coriander

chili

1 To make the dressing, mix together the yogurt, cucumber and seasoning in a bowl, then leave to chill while preparing and cooking the shrimp.

2 Peel the ginger, and chop it finely.

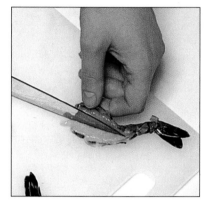

3 Prepare the shrimp by peeling off the shells, leaving the tails intact. Make a slit down the back of each shrimp and remove the black vein, then slit the shrimp completely down the back and open it out to make a "butterfly."

4 Heat the wok and dry-fry the peanuts, stirring constantly until golden brown. Leave to cool. Wipe out the wok with paper towels.

5 Heat the wok, add the oil and when hot add the ginger, garlic and chili. Stir-fry for 2–3 minutes until the garlic is softened but not brown.

6 Add the shrimp, then increase the heat and stir-fry for 1–2 minutes until the shrimp turn pink. Stir in the peanut butter and stir-fry for 2 minutes. Add the chopped coriander, then scatter in the peanuts. Garnish with coriander sprigs and serve with the cucumber dressing.

Steamed Spiced Pork and Water Chestnut Wontons

Ginger and Chinese five-spice powder flavor this version of steamed open dumplings – a favorite snack in many teahouses.

VARIATION

These can also be deep fried, in which case fold the edges over the filling to enclose it completely. Press well to seal. Deep-fry in batches in hot oil for about 2 minutes.

Makes about 36

INGREDIENTS
2 large Chinese cabbage leaves, plus extra for lining the steamer
2 scallions, finely chopped
½-in piece fresh ginger, finely chopped
2 oz canned water chestnuts (drained weight), rinsed and finely chopped
8oz ground pork
½ tsp Chinese five-spice powder
1 tbsp cornstarch
1 tbsp light soy sauce
1 tbsp Chinese rice wine
2 tsp sesame oil
generous pinch of sugar
about 36 wonton wrappers, each 3 in square
light soy sauce and hot chili oil, for dipping

1 Place the Chinese cabbage leaves one on top of another. Cut them lengthwise into quarters and then across into thin shreds.

2 Place the shredded Chinese cabbage leaves in a bowl. Add the scallions, ginger, water chestnuts, pork, five-spice powder, cornstarch, soy sauce, rice wine, sesame oil and sugar; mix well.

3 Set one wonton wrapper on a work surface. Place a heaped teaspoon of the filling in the center of the wrapper, then lightly dampen the edges with water.

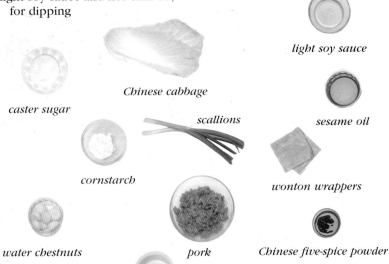

caster sugar

Chinese cabbage

light soy sauce

scallions

sesame oil

cornstarch

wonton wrappers

water chestnuts

pork

Chinese five-spice powder

Chinese rice wine

ginger

4 Lift the wrapper up around the filling, gathering to form a purse. Squeeze the wrapper firmly around the middle, then tap on the bottom to make a flat base. The top should be open. Place the wonton on a tray and cover with a damp dish towel.

5 Line the steamer with cabbage leaves and steam the dumplings for 12–15 minutes or until tender. Remove each batch from the steamer as soon as they are cooked, cover with foil and keep warm. Serve hot with soy sauce and chili oil for dipping.

Stir-fried Potatoes and Eggs

A bacon and egg breakfast dish done in true stir-fry style – fast and flavorful.

Serves 4

INGREDIENTS
12 oz cooked potatoes
3 tbsp olive oil
2 tsp fresh rosemary, chopped
pinch of freshly grated nutmeg
3 oz smoked bacon, cut into
   cubes
4 quail's eggs
salt flakes and freshly ground
   black pepper
fresh rosemary sprigs, to garnish

rosemary

*smoked
bacon*

quail's eggs

potato

1 Coarsely grate the potatoes and thoroughly pat dry on paper towels to remove all the moisture.

2 Heat the wok, then add 2 tbsp of oil. When the oil is hot, add the potatoes and cook them in batches until crisp and golden. This will take about 10 minutes. Drain the potatoes on paper towels, mix with the rosemary, nutmeg and seasoning and keep warm.

3 Add the bacon to the hot wok and stir-fry until crisp. Sprinkle the bacon on top of the potato, then season well.

4 Heat the wok, then add the remaining oil. When the oil is hot, fry the quail's eggs for about 2 minutes. Make a pile of the rosemary rosti, season it well, garnish with sprigs of fresh rosemary, then serve with the eggs.

Corn and Chicken Soup

This popular classic Chinese soup is delicious, and very easy to make.

Serves 4-6

INGREDIENTS

1 chicken breast fillet,
 about 4 oz, cubed
2 tsp light soy sauce
1 tbsp Chinese rice wine
1 tsp cornstarch
4 tbsp cold water
1 tsp sesame oil
2 tbsp peanut oil
1 tsp fresh ginger,
 finely grated
4 cups chicken stock, or
 bouillon cube and water
15-oz can cream-style corn
8-oz can corn kernels
2 eggs, beaten
2-3 scallions, green parts only,
 cut into tiny rounds
salt and ground black pepper

cornstarch

chicken stock

cream-style corn

chicken

corn kernels

egg

sesame oil

ginger

Chinese rice wine

1 Grind the chicken in a food processor, taking care not to over-process. Transfer the chicken to a bowl and stir in the soy sauce, rice wine, cornstarch, water, sesame oil and seasoning. Cover and leave for about 15 minutes to absorb the flavors.

2 Heat a wok over medium heat. Add the peanut oil and swirl it around. Add the ginger and stir-fry for a few seconds. Add the stock, creamed corn and corn kernels. Bring to just below boiling point.

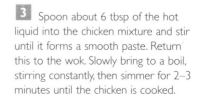

3 Spoon about 6 tbsp of the hot liquid into the chicken mixture and stir until it forms a smooth paste. Return this to the wok. Slowly bring to a boil, stirring constantly, then simmer for 2–3 minutes until the chicken is cooked.

4 Pour the beaten eggs into the soup in a slow steady stream, using a fork or chopsticks to stir the top of the soup in a figure-eight pattern. The egg should set in lacy shreds. Serve immediately with the scallions sprinkled over.

Vegetable Tempura

These deep-fried fritters are based on Kaki-age, a Japanese dish that often incorporates fish and shrimp as well as vegetables.

Makes 8

INGREDIENTS
2 medium zucchini
½ medium eggplant
1 large carrot
½ small Spanish onion
1 egg
½ cup ice water
1 cup all-purpose flour
salt and ground black pepper
vegetable oil,
   for deep-frying
sea salt flakes, lemon slices and
   Japanese soy sauce (*shoyu*),
   to serve

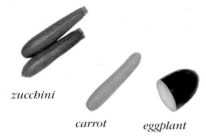

zucchini

carrot   *eggplant*

Spanish onion

all-purpose flour

egg   *vegetable oil*

1 Using a potato peeler, pare strips of peel from the zucchini and eggplant to give a striped effect.

2 Cut the zucchini, eggplant and carrot into strips about 3–4 in long and ⅛ in wide.

3 Put the zucchini, eggplant and carrot in a colander and sprinkle liberally with salt. Let stand for about 30 minutes, then rinse thoroughly under cold running water. Drain well.

4 Thinly slice the onion from top to base, discarding the plump pieces in the middle. Separate the layers so that there are lots of fine long strips. Mix all the vegetables together and season with salt and pepper.

5 Make the batter immediately before frying: mix the egg and iced water in a bowl, then sift in the flour. Mix very briefly using a fork or chopsticks. Do not overmix – the batter should remain lumpy. Add the vegetables to the batter and mix to combine.

6 Meanwhile, half-fill a wok with oil and heat to 350°F. Scoop up one heaped tablespoon of the mixture at a time and carefully lower into the oil. Deep-fry in batches for about 3 minutes, until golden brown and crisp. Drain on paper towels. Serve each diner with salt, lemon slices and a tiny bowl of Japanese soy sauce for dipping.

Crispy Spring Rolls with Sweet Chili Dipping Sauce

Miniature spring rolls make delicious appetizers or party finger food.

Makes 20-24

INGREDIENTS
1 oz rice vermicelli noodles
peanut oil
1 tsp fresh ginger,
   finely grated
2 scallions, finely shredded
2 oz carrot, finely shredded
2 oz snow peas, shredded
1 oz young spinach leaves
2 oz fresh beansprouts
1 tbsp fresh mint,
   finely chopped
1 tbsp fresh cilantro,
   finely chopped
2 tbsp Thai fish sauce (*nam pla*)
20-24 spring roll wrappers,
   each 5 in square
1 egg white, lightly beaten

FOR THE DIPPING SAUCE
4 tbsp sugar
¼ cup rice vinegar
2 fresh red chilies, seeded and
   finely chopped

noodles *spinach*

scallions

spring roll wrappers

Thai fish sauce *snow peas*

beansprouts *ginger* *carrot*

COOK'S TIP
You can cook the spring rolls for 2-3 hours in advance, then all you have to do is reheat them on a foil-lined baking sheet at 400°F for about 10 minutes.

1 First make the dipping sauce: place the sugar and vinegar in a small pan with 2 tbsp water. Heat gently, stirring until the sugar dissolves, then boil rapidly until it forms a light syrup. Stir in the chilies and leave to cool.

2 Soak the noodles according to the package instructions; rinse and drain well. Using scissors, snip the noodles into short lengths.

3 Heat a wok until hot. Add 1 tbsp oil and swirl it around. Add the ginger and scallions and stir-fry for 15 seconds. Add the carrot and snow peas and stir-fry for 2-3 minutes. Add the spinach, beansprouts, mint, cilantro, fish sauce and noodles and stir-fry for another minute. Set aside to cool.

4 Take one spring roll wrapper and arrange it so that it faces you in a diamond shape. Place a spoonful of filling just below the center, then fold up the bottom point over the filling.

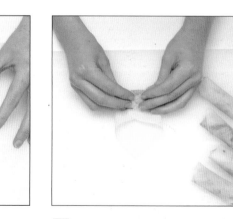

5 Fold in each side, then roll up tightly. Brush the end with beaten egg white to seal. Repeat until all the filling has been used.

6 Half-fill a wok with oil and heat to 350°F. Deep-fry the spring rolls in batches for 3-4 minutes, until golden and crisp. Drain on paper towels. Serve hot with the sweet chili dipping sauce.

Quick-fried Shrimp with Hot Spices

These spicy shrimp that cook in moments make a wonderful appetizer. Don't forget to provide your guests with finger bowls.

Serves 4

INGREDIENTS

1 lb large raw shrimp
1-in piece fresh ginger, grated
2 garlic cloves, crushed
1 tsp cayenne pepper
1 tsp ground turmeric
2 tsp black mustard seeds
seeds from 4 green cardamom pods, crushed
4 tbsp ghee or butter
½ cup coconut milk
2–3 tbsp chopped fresh cilantro
salt and ground black pepper
nan bread, to serve

shrimp

cilantro

coconut milk

cayenne

ghee

black mustard seeds

turmeric

ginger

garlic

cardamom pods

COOK'S TIP
If raw shrimp are unavailable, use cooked ones instead, but simmer gently in the coconut milk for just 1–2 minutes.

1 Peel the shrimp carefully, leaving the tails attached.

2 Using a small sharp knife, make a slit along the back of each shrimp and remove the dark vein. Rinse under cold running water, drain and pat dry.

3 Put the ginger, garlic, cayenne pepper, turmeric, mustard seeds and cardamom seeds in a bowl. Add the shrimp and toss to coat with the spices.

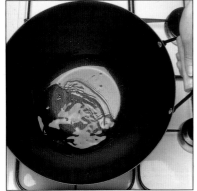

4 Heat a karahi or wok until hot. Add the ghee or butter and swirl it around until foaming.

5 Add the marinated shrimp and stir-fry for 1–1½ minutes, until they are just turning pink.

6 Stir in the coconut milk and simmer for 3–4 minutes, until the shrimp are cooked through. Season with salt and pepper. Sprinkle over the cilantro and serve at once with nan bread.

Shrimp Toasts

These crunchy sesame-topped toasts are simple to prepare using a food processor for the shrimp paste.

Makes 64

INGREDIENTS

8 ounces cooked, shelled shrimp, well
    drained and dried
1 egg white
2 green onions, chopped
1 teaspoon chopped fresh root ginger
1 garlic clove, chopped
1 teaspoon cornstarch
½ teaspoon salt
½ teaspoon sugar
2 to 3 dashes hot-pepper sauce
8 slices firm-textured white bread
4 to 5 tablespoons sesame seeds
vegetable oil for frying
green onion pompom, to garnish

bread

vegetable oil

egg white

sesame seeds

gingerroot

sugar

shrimp

cornstarch

garlic

green onions

hot-pepper sauce

1 Put the first 9 ingredients in the bowl of a food processor and process until the mixture forms a smooth paste, scraping down the side of the bowl occasionally.

2 Spread the shrimp paste evenly over the bread slices, then sprinkle over the sesame seeds, pressing to make them stick. Remove the crusts, then cut each slice diagonally into 4 triangles, then cut each in half again to make 64 in total.

3 Heat 2 inches vegetable oil in a heavy saucepan or wok, until hot but not smoking. Fry the shrimp-coated triangles for 30 to 60 seconds, turning once. Drain on paper towels and serve hot.

COOK'S TIP

You can prepare these in advance and heat them up in a hot oven before serving. Make sure they are crisp and properly heated through though; they won't be nearly as enjoyable if there isn't any crunch!

Thai-Fried Vegetables in Wonton Cups

These crispy cups are an ideal way to serve stir-fried vegetables; use your imagination to vary the fillings.

Makes 24

INGREDIENTS

2 tablespoons vegetable oil, plus extra
  for greasing
24 small wonton wrappers
½ cup hoisin sauce or plum sauce
  (optional)
1 teaspoon sesame oil
1 garlic clove, finely chopped
½-inch piece fresh gingerroot, finely
  chopped
2-inch piece of lemongrass, crushed
6 to 8 asparagus spears, cut into 1¼-
  inch pieces
8 to 10 ears baby corn, cut in half
  lengthwise
1 small red pepper, seeded and cut
  into short slivers
1 to 2 tablespoons sugar
2 tablespoons soy sauce
juice of 1 lime
1 to 2 teaspoons Chinese-style chili
  sauce (or to taste)
1 tsp *huac nam* or Thai or other fish
  sauce

lemongrass

red pepper

hoisin sauce

wonton wrappers

baby corn

vegetable oil

asparagus

sesame oil

soy sauce

lime

garlic

1 Preheat the oven to 350°F. Lightly grease twenty-four 1½-inch muffin cups. Press one wonton wrapper into each cup, turning the edges up to form a cup shape. Bake for 8 to 10 minutes until crisp and golden. Carefully remove to a wire rack to cool. If you like, brush each cup with a little hoisin or plum sauce (this will help keep the cups crisp if preparing them in advance).

2 In a wok or large skillet, heat 2 tablespoons vegetable oil and the sesame oil until very hot. Add the garlic, ginger, and lemongrass and stir-fry for 15 seconds until fragrant. Add the asparagus, corn, and red pepper pieces and stir-fry for 2 minutes until tender crisp.

3 Add the sugar, soy sauce, lime juice, chili sauce, and fish sauce and toss well to coat. Stir-fry for 30 seconds longer.

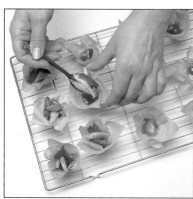

4 Spoon an equal amount of vegetable mixture into each of the prepared wonton cups and serve hot.

Hot Spicy Crab Claws

Crab claws are used to delicious effect in this quick appetizer based on an Indonesian dish called *Kepiting Pedas*.

Serves 4

INGREDIENTS
12 fresh or frozen and thawed
    cooked crab claws
4 shallots, coarsely chopped
2-4 fresh red chilies, seeded and
    coarsely chopped
3 garlic cloves, coarsely chopped
1 tsp grated fresh ginger
½ tsp ground coriander
3 tbsp peanut oil
60 ml/4 tbsp water
10 ml/2 tsp sweet soy sauce
    (*kecap manis*)
2-3 tsp lime juice
salt, to taste
fresh coriander, to garnish

shallots

crab claws

sweet soy sauce

garlic

coriander

red chilies

peanut oil

lime

ginger

1 Crack the crab claws with the back of a heavy knife to make eating easier. Set aside. In a mortar, pound the chopped shallots with the pestle until pulpy. Add the chilies, garlic, ginger and ground coriander and pound until the mixture forms a coarse paste.

2 Heat the wok over medium heat. Add the oil and swirl it around. When it is hot, stir in the chili paste. Stir-fry for about 30 seconds. Increase the heat to high. Add the crab claws and stir-fry for another 3–4 minutes.

3 Stir in the water, sweet soy sauce, lime juice and salt to taste. Continue to stir-fry for 1–2 minutes. Serve at once, garnished with fresh cilantro. The crab claws are eaten with the fingers, so provide finger bowls.

COOK'S TIP
If whole crab claws are unavailable, look out for frozen prepared crab claws. These are shelled with just the tip of the claw attached to the white meat. Stir-fry for about two minutes until heated through.

Thai Seafood Salad

This seafood salad with chili, lemongrass and fish sauce is light and refreshing.

Serves 4

INGREDIENTS
8 oz cleaned squid
8 oz raw large shrimp
8 sea scallops, whole
8 oz firm white fish
2–3 tbsp olive oil
small mixed lettuce leaves and
  cilantro sprigs, to serve

FOR THE DRESSING
2 small fresh red chilies, seeded
  and finely chopped
2-in piece lemongrass,
  finely chopped
2 fresh kaffir lime leaves,
  shredded
2 tbsp Thai fish sauce
  (*nam pla*)
2 shallots, thinly sliced
2 tbsp lime juice
2 tbsp rice vinegar
2 tsp sugar

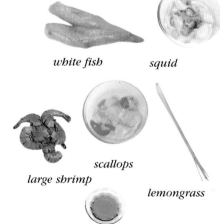

white fish   *squid*

scallops

large shrimp

lemongrass

Thai fish sauce

shallots   *kaffir lime leaves*

1 Prepare the seafood: slit open the squid bodies, score the flesh with a sharp knife, then cut into square pieces. Halve the tentacles, if necessary. Peel and devein the shrimp. Cut the sea scallops in half (if using bay scallops, leave whole). Cube the white fish.

2 Heat a wok until hot. Add the oil and swirl it around, then add the shrimp and stir-fry for 2–3 minutes until pink. Transfer to a large bowl. Stir-fry the squid and scallops for 1–2 minutes, until opaque. Remove and add to the shrimp. Stir-fry the white fish for 2–3 minutes. Remove and add to the cooked seafood. Reserve any juices.

3 Put all the dressing ingredients in a small bowl with the reserved juices from the wok; mix well.

4 Pour the dressing over the seafood and toss gently. Arrange the salad leaves and cilantro sprigs on four individual plates, then spoon the seafood on top. Serve at once.

Salmon Teriyaki

Marinating the salmon makes it so wonderfully tender, it just melts in the mouth, and the crunchy condiment provides an excellent foil. If you are short of time, you can buy good ready-made teriyaki sauce in a bottle.

Serves 4

INGREDIENTS
1½ lb salmon fillet
1 tsp salt
2 tbsp sunflower oil
watercress, to garnish

FOR THE TERIYAKI SAUCE
1 tsp superfine sugar
1 tsp dry white wine
1 tsp rice wine or dry sherry
2 tbsp dark soy sauce

FOR THE CONDIMENT
2 in piece ginger root, peeled
    and grated
few drops of pink food coloring
2 oz jicama, grated

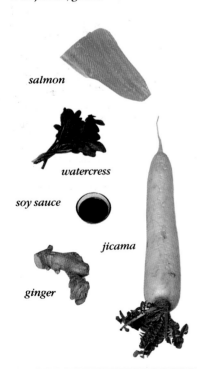

salmon

watercress

soy sauce

jicama

ginger

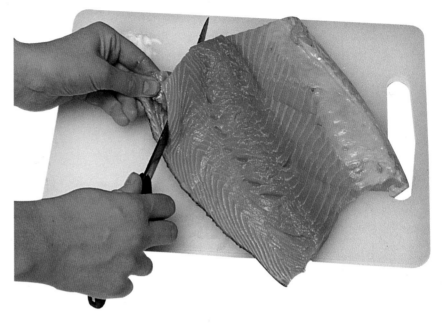

1 Mix all the teriyaki sauce ingredients together until the sugar dissolves.

2 To remove the skin from the salmon, sprinkle the salt over the chopping board to prevent the fish slipping, then use a very sharp fish filleting knife.

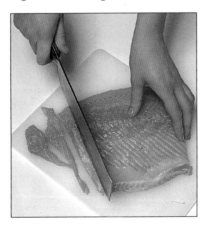

3 Cut the fillet into strips, then place it in a non-metallic dish. Pour the teriyaki sauce over the fish and leave to marinate for 10–15 minutes.

4 To make the condiment, place the ginger in a bowl, mix in the food coloring, then stir in the jicama.

5 Lift the salmon from the teriyaki sauce and drain.

6 Heat the wok, then add the oil. When the oil is hot, add the salmon and stir-fry in batches for 3–4 minutes until the fish is cooked. Garnish with watercress and serve with the jicama and ginger condiment.

Fish Balls with Chinese Greens

These tasty fish balls are easy to make using a food processor. Here they are partnered with a selection of green vegetables – bok choy is available at most Asian stores.

Serves 4

INGREDIENTS
FOR THE FISH BALLS
1 lb white fish fillets, skinned, boned and cubed
3 scallions, chopped
1 slice Canadian bacon, rinded and chopped
1 tbsp Chinese rice wine
2 tbsp light soy sauce
1 egg white

FOR THE VEGETABLES
1 small head bok choy
1 tsp cornstarch
1 tbsp light soy sauce
⅔ cup fish stock
2 tbsp peanut oil
2 garlic cloves, sliced
1-in piece fresh ginger, cut into thin shreds
3 oz green beans
6 oz snow peas
3 scallions, sliced diagonally into 2–3-in lengths
salt and ground black pepper

garlic

ginger

scallions

bacon

light soy sauce

snow peas

bok choy

green beans

fish stock

Chinese rice wine

peanut oil

fish fillets

1 Put the fish, scallions, bacon, rice wine, soy sauce and egg white in a food processor. Process until smooth. With wetted hands, form the mixture into about 24 small balls.

2 Steam the fish balls in batches in a lightly greased bamboo steamer in a wok for 5–10 minutes until firm. Remove from the steamer and keep warm.

3 Meanwhile, trim the bok choy, removing any discolored leaves or damaged stems, then tear into manageable pieces.

4 In a small bowl blend together the cornstarch, soy sauce and stock.

VARIATION
Replace the snow peas and green beans with broccoli florets. Blanch them before stir-frying.

5 Heat a wok until hot, add the oil and swirl it around. Add the garlic and ginger and stir-fry for 1 minute. Add the beans and stir-fry for 2–3 minutes, then add the snow peas, scallions and pak choi. Stir-fry for 2–3 minutes.

6 Add the sauce to the wok and cook, stirring, until it has thickened and the vegetables are tender but crisp. Taste and adjust the seasoning, if necessary. Serve at once with the fish balls.

Lemongrass-and-basil-scented Mussels

Thai flavorings of lemongrass and basil are used in this quick and easy dish.

Serves 4

INGREDIENTS
4–4½ lb fresh mussels
   in the shell
2 lemongrass stalks
handful of small fresh basil leaves
2-in piece fresh ginger
2 shallots, finely chopped
¼ pint/⅔ cup fish stock

lemongrass

mussels

fish stock

shallots

ginger

basil

1 Scrub the mussels under cold running water, scraping off any barnacles with a small sharp knife. Pull or cut off the hairy "beards". Discard any with damaged shells and any that remain open when sharply tapped.

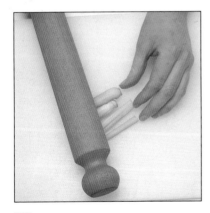

2 Cut each lemongrass stalk in half and bruise with a rolling pin.

COOK'S TIP
Mussels are best bought fresh and eaten on the day of purchase. Any that remain closed after cooking should be thrown away.

3 Coarsely chop half the basil leaves; reserve the remainder for the garnish.

4 Put the mussels, lemongrass, chopped basil, ginger, shallots and stock in a wok. Bring to a boil, cover and simmer for 5 minutes. Discard any mussels that remain closed. Sprinkle over the reserved basil and serve at once.

Spicy Fish Fritters

These crispy, spicy fritters are based on a dish from Baltistan, India.

Serves 4

INGREDIENTS
2 tsp cumin seeds
2 tsp coriander seeds
1–2 dried red chilies
2 tbsp vegetable oil
1½ cups gram flour
1 tsp salt
2 tsp garam masala
1 cup water
peanut oil, for deep-frying
1½ lb fish fillets, such as cod,
   skinned, boned and cut into
   thick strips
mint sprigs and lime halves,
   to garnish

fish fillets

peanut oil

gram flour

red chilies

vegetable oil

coriander

garam masala

1 Crush the cumin, coriander and chili(es), using a mortar and pestle. Heat the vegetable oil in a kadhai or wok and stir-fry the spices for 1–2 minutes.

2 Put the gram flour, salt, spice mixture and garam masala in a bowl. Gradually stir in enough water to make a thick batter. Cover and allow to rest for 30 minutes.

3 Half-fill a kadhai or wok with peanut oil and heat to 375°F. When the oil is ready, dip the fish, just a few pieces at a time, into the batter, shaking off any excess.

4 Deep-fry the fish in batches for 4–5 minutes, until golden brown. Drain on paper towels. Serve immediately, garnished with mint sprigs and lime halves for squeezing over the fritters.

Red Snapper with Ginger and Scallions

This is a classic Chinese way of cooking fish. Pouring the oil slowly over the scallions and ginger allows it to partially cook them, enhancing their flavor.

Serves 2-3

INGREDIENTS
1 red snapper, about
    1½-2 lb, cleaned and scaled
    with head left on
1 bunch scallions, cut into thin
    shreds
1-in piece fresh ginger, cut into
    thin shreds
¼ tsp salt
¼ tsp sugar
3 tbsp peanut oil
1 tsp sesame oil
2-3 tbsp light soy sauce
scallion brushes, to garnish

scallions

ginger

peanut oil

sesame oil

red snapper

light soy sauce

sugar

COOK'S TIP
If the fish is too big to fit inside the steamer, cut off the head and place it alongside the body, which can then be reassembled after it is cooked for serving.

1 Rinse the fish, then pat dry with paper towels. Slash the flesh diagonally, three times on each side. Set the fish on a heatproof oval plate that will fit inside your bamboo steamer.

2 Tuck about one-third of the scallions and ginger inside the body cavity. Place the plate inside the steamer, cover with its lid, then place in a wok.

3 Steam over medium heat for 10–15 minutes, until the fish flakes easily when tested with the tip of a knife.

4 Carefully remove the plate from the steamer. Sprinkle over the salt, sugar and remaining scallions and ginger.

5 Heat the oils in a small pan until very hot, then slowly pour over the fish.

6 Drizzle over the soy sauce and serve at once, garnished with scallion brushes.

Stir-fried Squid with Black Bean Sauce

If you cannot buy fresh squid you will certainly find small or baby frozen squid, skinned, boned and with heads removed, at your local fishmonger.

Serves 4

INGREDIENTS
½ lb fresh or frozen squid
1 red chili
2 tsp peanut oil
1 clove garlic, crushed
2 tbsp black bean sauce
4 tbsp water
fresh parsley sprigs, to garnish
steamed rice, to serve

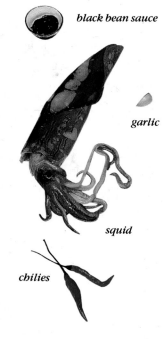

black bean sauce

garlic

squid

chilies

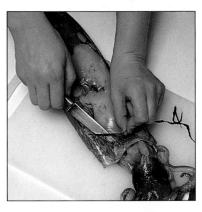

1 Carefully remove the skin from the squid and discard.

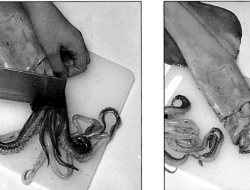

2 Cut off the head of each squid just below the eye, and discard.

3 Remove the bone from the squid and discard.

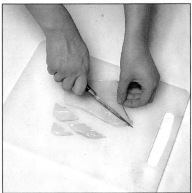

4 Cut the squid into bite-size pieces and score the flesh in a criss-cross pattern with a sharp knife.

5 Carefully deseed the chili and chop it finely. Wear rubber gloves to protect your hands if necessary.

6 Heat the wok, then add the oil. When the oil is hot, add the garlic and cook until it starts to sizzle but does not color. Stir in the squid and fry until the flesh starts to stiffen and turn white. Quickly stir in the black bean sauce, water and chili. Continue stirring until the squid is cooked and tender (not more than a minute). Garnish with parsley sprigs and the tentacles and serve with steamed rice.

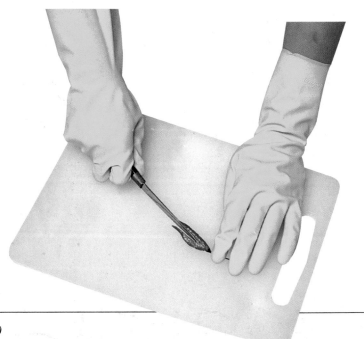

Green Seafood Curry

This curry is based on a Thai classic. The lovely green color is imparted by the finely chopped chili and fresh herbs added during the last few moments of cooking.

COOK'S TIP
If you like more fiery curries, increase the amount of green curry paste used.

Serves 4

INGREDIENTS
8 oz small, cleaned squid
8 oz raw large shrimp
1¾ cups coconut milk
2 tbsp green curry paste
2 fresh kaffir lime leaves, finely shredded
2 tbsp Thai fish sauce (*nam pla*)
1 lb firm white fish fillets, skinned, boned and cut into chunks
2 fresh green chilies, seeded and finely chopped
2 tbsp torn basil or cilantro leaves
squeeze of lime juice
Thai jasmine rice, to serve

shrimp

green chilies

squid

white fish

basil

coconut milk

green curry paste

kaffir lime leaves

1 Rinse the squid and pat dry with paper towels. Cut the bodies into rings and halve the tentacles, if necessary.

2 Heat a wok until hot, add the shrimp and stir-fry without any oil for about 4 minutes, until they turn pink.

3 Remove the shrimp from the heat and when they are cool enough to handle, peel off the shells. Make a slit along the back of each one and remove the black vein.

4 Pour the coconut milk into the wok, then bring to a boil, stirring. Add the curry paste, shredded lime leaves and fish sauce. Reduce the heat to a simmer and cook for about 10 minutes, enough for the flavors to develop.

5 Add the squid, shrimp and white fish and cook for about 2 minutes until the seafood is tender. Take care not to overcook the squid, as it will become tough very quickly.

6 Just before serving, stir in the chilies and basil or cilantro. Taste and adjust the flavor with a squeeze of lime juice. Serve with Thai jasmine rice.

Spiced Shrimp with Coconut

This spicy dish is based on *Sambal Goreng Udang*, which is Indonesian in origin. It is best served with plain boiled rice.

Serves 3-4

INGREDIENTS
2-3 fresh red chilies, seeded
    and chopped
3 shallots, chopped
1 lemongrass stalk, chopped
2 garlic cloves, chopped
thin sliver of dried shrimp paste
½ tsp ground galangal
1 tsp ground turmeric
1 tsp ground coriander
1 tbsp peanut oil
1 cup water
2 fresh kaffir lime leaves
1 tsp light brown sugar
2 tomatoes, peeled, seeded
    and chopped
1 cup coconut milk
1½ lb large raw shrimp,
    peeled and deveined
squeeze of lemon juice
salt, to taste
shredded scallions and
    flaked coconut, to garnish

1 In a mortar pound the chilies, shallots, lemongrass, garlic, shrimp paste, galangal, turmeric and coriander with a pestle until it forms a paste.

lemongrass

garlic

dried shrimp paste

turmeric

red chilies

shrimp

coriander

peanut oil

coconut milk   *sugar*

galangal

tomatoes

shallots

kaffir lime leaves

COOK'S TIP
Dried shrimp paste, much used in Southeast Asia, is available at Asian stores.

2 Heat a wok until hot, add the oil and swirl it around. Add the spiced paste and stir-fry for about 2 minutes. Pour in the water and add the kaffir lime leaves, sugar and tomatoes. Simmer for 8–10 minutes, until most of the liquid has evaporated.

3 Add the coconut milk and shrimp and cook gently, stirring, for about 4 minutes until the shrimp are pink. Taste and adjust the seasoning with salt and a squeeze of lemon juice. Serve at once, garnished with shredded scallions and toasted flaked coconut.

Sea Bass with Chinese Chives

Chinese chives are widely available in Oriental supermarkets but if you are unable to buy them, use half a large Spanish onion, finely sliced, instead.

Serves 4

INGREDIENTS

4 sea bass fillets, about 1 lb in all
1 tsp cornstarch
3 tbsp vegetable oil
6 oz/2 cups Chinese chives
1 tbsp rice wine
1 tsp superfine sugar
salt and freshly ground black pepper
Chinese chives with flowerheads,
    to garnish
mixed lettuce salad, to serve

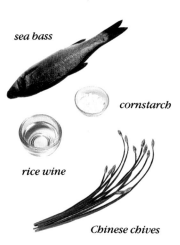

sea bass

cornstarch

rice wine

Chinese chives

1 Remove the scales from the bass by scraping the fillets with the back of a knife, working from tail end to head end.

2 Cut the fillets into large chunks and dust them lightly with cornstarch, salt and pepper.

3 Heat the wok, then add 2 tbsp of the oil. When the oil is hot, toss the chunks of fish in the wok briefly to seal, then set aside. Wipe out the wok with paper towels.

4 Cut the Chinese chives into 2 in lengths and discard the flowers. Heat the wok and add the remaining oil, then stir-fry the Chinese chives for 30 seconds. Add the fish and rice wine, then bring to the boil and stir in the sugar. Serve hot, garnished with some flowering Chinese chives, and with a side dish of crisp mixed green salad.

Fragrant Swordfish with Ginger and Lemon Grass

Swordfish is a meaty fish which cooks well in a wok if it has been marinated as a steak rather than in strips. If you cannot get swordfish, use tuna.

Serves 4

INGREDIENTS
1 kaffir lime leaf
3 tbsp kosher salt
5 tbsp brown sugar
4 swordfish steaks, about 8 oz each
1 stalk lemon grass, sliced
1 in piece ginger root, cut into
    matchsticks
1 lime
1 tbsp grapeseed oil
1 large ripe avocado, peeled and
    pitted
salt and freshly ground black pepper

avocado

ginger

lemon grass

lime

lime leaf

swordfish steak

1 Bruise the lime leaf by crushing slightly, to release the flavor.

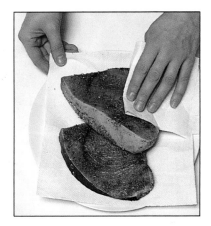

2 To make the marinade, process the kosher salt, brown sugar and lime leaf together in a food processor until thoroughly blended.

3 Place the swordfish steaks in a bowl. Sprinkle the marinade over them and add the lemon grass and ginger. Leave for 3–4 hours to marinate.

4 Rinse off the marinade and pat dry with paper towels.

5 Peel the lime. Remove any excess pith from the peel, then cut into very thin strips.

6 Heat the wok, then add the oil. When the oil is hot, add the lime rind and then the fish steaks, and stir-fry for 3–4 minutes. Add the juice of the lime. Remove from the heat, slice the avocado and add to the fish. Season and serve.

Squid with Peppers in Black Bean Sauce

Salted black beans add a traditionally Chinese flavor to this tasty stir-fry.

Serves 4

INGREDIENTS

2 tbsp salted black beans
2 tbsp medium-dry sherry
1 tbsp light soy sauce
1 tsp cornstarch
½ tsp sugar
2 tbsp water
3 tbsp peanut oil
1 lb cleaned squid, scored and
    cut into thick strips
1 tsp finely chopped
    fresh ginger
1 garlic clove, finely chopped
1 fresh green chili,
    seeded and sliced
6–8 scallions, cut diagonally
    into 1-in lengths
½ red and ½ green bell pepper,
    cored seeded and cut into
    1-in diamonds
3 oz shiitake mushrooms,
    thickly sliced

scallions

shiitake mushrooms

medium-dry sherry

light soy sauce

ginger

red pepper

squid

salted black beans   *green pepper*

green chili

1 Rinse and finely chop the black beans. Place them in a bowl with the sherry, soy sauce, cornstarch, sugar and water; mix well.

2 Heat a wok until hot, add the oil and swirl it around. When the oil is very hot, add the squid and stir-fry for 1–1½ minutes, until opaque and curled at the edges. Remove with a slotted spoon and set aside.

3 Add the ginger, garlic and chili to the wok and stir-fry for a few seconds. Then add the scallions, peppers and mushrooms, then stir-fry for 2 minutes.

4 Return the squid to the wok with the sauce. Cook, stirring, for about 1 minute, until thickened. Serve at once.

Spicy Crab and Coconut

This spicy dish is delicious served with plain warm Naan bread.

Serves 4

INGREDIENTS

1½ oz dried unsweetened shredded coconut
2 cloves garlic
2 in piece ginger root, peeled and grated
½ tsp cumin seeds
1 small stick cinnamon
½ tsp ground turmeric
2 dried red chilies
1 tbsp coriander seeds
½ tsp poppy seeds
1 tbsp vegetable oil
1 medium onion, sliced
1 small green pepper, cut into strips
16 crab claws
fresh coriander sprigs, crushed, to garnish
⅔ cup natural low-fat yogurt, to serve

pepper

cumin seeds

cinnamon

crab claw

1 Place the shredded coconut, garlic, ginger, cumin seeds, cinnamon, turmeric, red chilies, coriander and poppy seeds into a food processor and process until well blended.

2 Heat the oil in the wok and fry the onion until soft, but not colored.

3 Stir in the green pepper and stir-fry for 1 minute.

4 Remove the vegetables with a slotted spoon and heat the wok. Add the crab claws, stir-fry for 2 minutes, then briefly return all the spiced vegetables to the wok. Garnish with fresh coriander sprigs and serve with the cooling yogurt.

Sweet-and-sour Fish

The combination of sweet and sour is a popular one in many cuisines. The sauce can be made up to two days in advance.

Serves 3-4

INGREDIENTS

1 lb white fish fillets, skinned, boned and cubed
½ tsp Chinese five-spice powder
1 tsp light soy sauce
1 egg, lightly beaten
2-3 tbsp cornstarch
peanut oil, for deep-frying

FOR THE SAUCE

2 tsp cornstarch
4 tbsp water
4 tbsp pineapple juice
3 tbsp Chinese rice vinegar
3 tbsp sugar
2 tsp light soy sauce
2 tbsp tomato ketchup
2 tsp Chinese rice wine or medium-dry sherry
3 tbsp peanut oil
1 garlic clove, crushed
1 tbsp finely chopped fresh ginger
6 scallions, sliced diagonally into 2-in lengths
1 green bell pepper, seeded and cut into ¾-in pieces
4 oz fresh pineapple, cut into ¾-in pieces
salt and ground black pepper

light soy sauce

white fish

scallion

garlic

cornstarch

egg

green pepper

Chinese rice wine

ginger

tomato ketchup

Chinese five-spice powder

pineapple

1 Put the fish in a bowl. Sprinkle over the five-spice powder and soy sauce, then toss gently. Cover and allow to marinate for about 30 minutes. Dip the fish in the egg, then in the cornstarch, shaking off any excess.

2 Half-fill a wok with oil and heat to 375°F. Deep-fry the fish in batches for about 2 minutes, until golden. Drain and keep warm. Carefully pour off all the oil from the wok and wipe clean.

4 Heat the wok until hot, add 2 tbsp of the oil and swirl it around. Add the garlic and ginger and stir-fry for a few seconds. Add the scallions and green pepper and stir-fry over medium heat for 2 minutes. Add the pineapple.

3 To make the sauce, blend together in a bowl the cornstarch, water, pineapple juice, rice vinegar, sugar, soy sauce, ketchup and rice wine or sherry. Mix well, then set aside.

5 Pour in the sauce and cook, stirring until thickened. Stir in the remaining 1 tbsp oil and add seasoning to taste. Pour the sauce over the fish and serve at once.

Thai Fish Stir-fry

This is a substantial dish: it is best served with chunks of fresh crusty white bread, for mopping up all the delicious, spicy juices.

Serves 4

INGREDIENTS
1½ lb mixed seafood (for example, red snapper, cod, raw shrimp), filleted and skinned
1¼ cups coconut milk
1 tbsp vegetable oil
salt and freshly ground black pepper

FOR THE SAUCE
2 large red chilies
1 onion, roughly chopped
2 in piece ginger root, peeled and sliced
2 in piece lemon grass, outer leaf discarded, roughly sliced
2 in piece galingale, peeled and sliced
6 blanched almonds, chopped
½ tsp turmeric
½ tsp salt

chili

onion

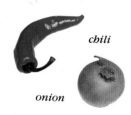

ginger

shrimp

1 Cut the filleted fish into large chunks. Peel the shrimp, keeping their tails intact.

2 Carefully remove the seeds from the chilies and chop roughly, wearing rubber gloves to protect your hands if necessary. Then, make the sauce by putting the chilies and the other sauce ingredients in the food processor with 3 tbsp of the coconut milk. Blend until smooth.

3 Heat the wok, then add the oil. When the oil is hot, stir-fry the seafood for 2–3 minutes, then remove.

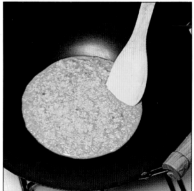

4 Add the sauce and the remaining coconut milk to the wok, then return the seafood. Bring to the boil, season well and serve with crusty bread.

Spiced Scallops in their Shells

Scallops are excellent steamed. When served with this spicy sauce, they make a delicious yet simple appetizer. Each person spoons sauce onto the scallops before eating them.

Serves 4

INGREDIENTS

8 scallops, shelled (the shells are available in cooking ware stores and some good fish markets)
2 slices fresh ginger, finely shredded
½ garlic clove, shredded
2 scallions, green parts only, shredded
salt and pepper

FOR THE SAUCE

1 garlic clove, crushed
1 tbsp fresh ginger, finely grated
2 scallions, white parts only, chopped
1-2 fresh green chilies, seeded and finely chopped
1 tbsp light soy sauce
1 tbsp dark soy sauce
2 tsp sesame oil

scallops

ginger

scallions

garlic

light soy sauce

green chili

dark soy sauce

sesame oil

1 Remove the dark beard-like fringe and tough muscle from the scallops.

2 Place 2 scallops in each shell. Season lightly with salt and pepper, then sprinkle the ginger, garlic and scallions on top. Place the shells in a bamboo steamer and steam for about 6 minutes, until the scallops look opaque (you may have to do this in batches).

3 Meanwhile, mix together all the sauce ingredients and pour into a small serving bowl.

4 Carefully remove each shell from the steamer, taking care not to spill the juices, and arrange them on a serving plate with the sauce bowl in the center. Serve at once.

Pan-fried Red Snapper with Lemon

This spectacularly attractive and delicious dish is well worth the time it takes to prepare.

Serves 4

INGREDIENTS
1 large bulb fennel
1 lemon
12 red snapper fillets, skin left intact
3 tbsp fresh marjoram, chopped
3 tbsp olive oil
8 oz/3 cups lamb's lettuce or
    Bibb lettuce
salt and freshly ground black pepper

FOR THE VINAIGRETTE
generous ¾ cup peanut oil
1 tbsp white wine vinegar
1 tbsp sherry vinegar
salt and freshly ground black pepper,
    to taste

FOR THE SAUCE
1½ oz black olives, pitted
1 tbsp unsalted butter
1 tbsp capers

fennel

red snapper

marjoram

lamb's lettuce

1 Trim the fennel bulb and cut it into fine matchsticks. Peel the lemon. Remove any excess pith from the peel, then cut it into fine strips. Blanch the rind and refresh it immediately in cold water. Drain.

2 Make the vinaigrette by placing all the ingredients in a small bowl and lightly whisking until well mixed.

3 Sprinkle the red snapper fillets with salt, pepper and marjoram.

4 Heat the wok and add the olive oil. When the oil is very hot, add the fennel and stir-fry for 1 minute, then drain and remove.

5 Reheat the wok and, when the oil is hot, stir-fry the red snapper fillets, cooking them skin-side down first for 2 minutes, then flipping them over for 1 further minute. Drain well on paper towels and wipe the wok clean with paper towels.

6 For the sauce, cut the olives into slivers. Heat the wok and add the butter. When the butter is hot, stir-fry the capers and olives for about 1 minute. Toss the lettuce in the dressing. Arrange the fillets on a bed of lettuce, topped with the fennel and lemon, and serve with the olive and caper sauce.

Spiced Salmon Stir-fry

Marinating the salmon allows all the flavors to develop, and the lime tenderizes the fish beautifully, so it needs very little stir-frying – be careful not to overcook it.

Serves 4

INGREDIENTS
4 salmon steaks, about 8 oz each
4 whole star anise
2 stalks lemon grass, sliced
juice of 3 limes
rind of 3 limes, finely grated
2 tbsp honey
2 tbsp grapeseed oil
salt and freshly ground black pepper
lime wedges, to garnish

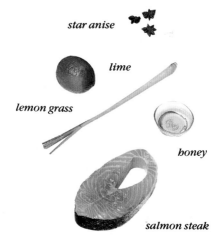

star anise

lime

lemon grass

honey

salmon steak

COOK'S TIP

Always dry off any marinade from meat, fish or vegetables to ensure that the hot oil does not splutter when you add them to the wok.

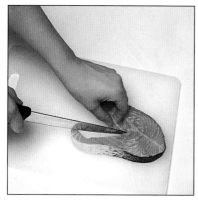

1 Remove the middle bone from each steak, using a very sharp filleting knife, to make two strips from each steak.

2 Remove the skin by inserting the knife at the thin end of each piece of salmon. Sprinkle 1 tsp salt on the cutting board to prevent the fish slipping while you remove the skin. Slice into pieces using diagonal cuts.

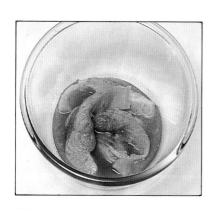

3 Coarsely crush the star anise in a pestle and mortar. Marinate the salmon in a non-metallic dish, with the star anise, lemon grass, lime juice and rind and honey. Season well with salt and pepper, cover and chill overnight.

4 Carefully drain the salmon from the marinade, pat dry on paper towels, and reserve the marinade.

5 Heat the wok, then add the oil. When the oil is hot, add the salmon and stir-fry, stirring constantly until cooked. Increase the heat, pour over the marinade and bring to a boil. Garnish with lime wedges and serve.

Oriental Scallops with Ginger Relish

If possible, buy scallops in their shells to be sure of their freshness; your fishmonger will open them for you if you find this difficult to do. Some specialty fishmongers will sell scallops with their roe.

Serves 4

INGREDIENTS
8 sea scallops
4 whole star anise
2 tbsp unsalted butter
salt and freshly ground white pepper
fresh chervil sprigs and whole star
    anise, to garnish

FOR THE RELISH
½ cucumber, peeled
salt, for sprinkling
2 in piece ginger root, peeled
2 tsp superfine sugar
3 tbsp rice wine vinegar
2 tsp ginger juice, strained from a jar
of preserved ginger
sesame seeds, for sprinkling

ginger

chervil

scallop

star anise

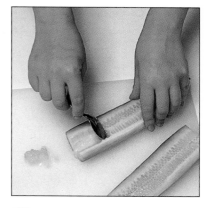

1 To make the relish, halve the cucumber lengthwise and scoop out the seeds with a teaspoon.

2 Cut the cucumber into 1 in pieces, place in a colander and sprinkle liberally with salt. Set aside for 30 minutes.

3 To prepare the scallops, cut each into 2–3 slices. Coarsely grind the star anise in a pestle and mortar.

4 Place the scallop slices with the roe in a bowl and marinate with the star anise and seasoning for about 1 hour.

5 Rinse the cucumber under cold water and pat dry on paper towels. Cut the ginger into thin julienne strips and mix with the remaining relish ingredients. Cover and chill until needed.

6 Heat the wok and add the butter. When the butter is hot, add the scallop slices and stir-fry for 2–3 minutes. Garnish with sprigs of chervil and whole star anise, and serve with the cucumber relish, sprinkled with sesame seeds.

Chicken Liver Stir-fry

The final sprinkling of lemon, parsley and garlic granita gives this dish a delightful fresh flavor and wonderful aroma.

Serves 4

INGREDIENTS
1¼ lb chicken livers
6 tbsp butter
6 oz field mushrooms
2 oz chanterelle mushrooms
3 cloves garlic, finely chopped
2 shallots, finely chopped
⅔ cup medium sherry
3 fresh rosemary sprigs
2 tbsp fresh parsley, chopped
rind of 1 lemon, grated
salt and freshly ground pepper
fresh rosemary sprigs, to garnish
4 thick slices of white toast, to serve

1 Clean and trim the chicken livers to remove any gristle or muscle.

2 Season the livers generously with salt and freshly ground black pepper, tossing well to coat thoroughly.

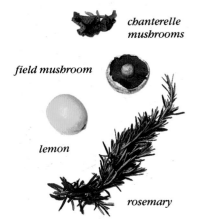

chanterelle mushrooms

field mushroom

lemon

rosemary

3 Heat the wok and add 1 tbsp of the butter. When melted, add the livers in batches (melting more butter where necessary but reserving 2 tbsp for the vegetables) and flash-fry until golden brown. Drain with a slotted spoon and transfer to a plate, then place in a low oven to keep warm.

4 Cut the field mushrooms into thick slices and, depending on the size of the chanterelles, cut in half.

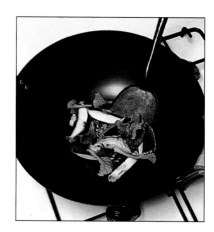

5 Heat the wok and add the remaining butter. When melted, stir in two-thirds of the chopped garlic and the shallots and stir-fry for 1 minute until golden brown. Stir in the mushrooms and continue to cook for a further 2 minutes.

6 Add the sherry, bring to a boil and simmer for 2–3 minutes until syrupy. Add the rosemary, salt and pepper and return livers to the pan. Stir-fry for 1 minute. Garnish with extra sprigs of rosemary, and serve sprinkled with a mixture of lemon, parsley and the remaining chopped garlic, with slices of toast.

Beef Rendang

In this curry from Indonesia, the meat is simmered in a mixture of coconut milk and spices until the liquid has almost disappeared, leaving dark, intensely flavored meat.

COOK'S TIP
This curry tastes even better if made the day before and kept covered in the fridge. Reheat it on top of the stove until piping hot before serving.

Serves 4

INGREDIENTS
4 dried red chilies
3-in piece galangal
6 shallots, chopped
1 small red bell pepper, seeded and chopped
4 garlic cloves, chopped
2 tsp ground cinnamon
2 tsp ground coriander
1 tsp ground turmeric
1 tsp ground cloves
1 tbsp peanut oil
6¼ cups coconut milk
2 bay leaves
2 lemongrass stalks, bruised
3 fresh kaffir lime leaves
2¼ lb round or flank steak, trimmed and cut into 2-in cubes
1 tsp salt
shredded kaffir lime leaves and red chili flowers, to garnish
plain boiled rice, to serve

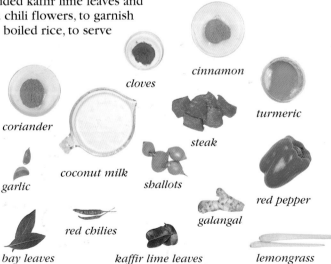

coriander *cloves* *cinnamon* *turmeric* *coconut milk* *steak* *shallots* *garlic* *red chilies* *galangal* *red pepper* *bay leaves* *kaffir lime leaves* *lemongrass*

1 Crumble or break the chilies into a bowl. Add 4 tbsp water and allow to soak for 30 minutes.

2 Peel and thickly chop the galangal.

3 Put the soaked chilies and their liquid, the galangal, the chopped shallots, pepper, garlic and remaining spices into a blender or food processor and blend until smooth.

4 Heat a wok until hot, add the oil and swirl it around. Add the spice paste and stir-fry for about 2 minutes. Pour in the coconut milk and add the bay leaves, lemongrass and kaffir lime leaves. Bring to a boil, stirring constantly.

5 Add the meat and salt. Reduce the heat and simmer, uncovered for 2–2½ hours, stirring occasionally, until most of the liquid has evaporated. Towards the end of cooking, stir the meat more frequently to prevent it sticking. Taste and season if necessary. Garnish with shredded kaffir lime leaves and red chili flowers. Serve with plain boiled rice.

Paper-thin Lamb with Scallions

Scallions lend a delicious flavor to the lamb in this simple supper dish.

Serves 3-4

INGREDIENTS

1 lb lamb cutlet
2 tbsp Chinese rice wine
2 tsp light soy sauce
½ tsp roasted and ground
  Szechuan peppercorns
½ tsp salt
½ tsp dark brown sugar
4 tsp dark soy sauce
1 tbsp sesame oil
2 tbsp peanut oil
2 garlic cloves, thinly sliced
2 bunches scallions, cut
  into 3-in lengths,
  then shredded
30 ml/2 tbsp chopped
  fresh cilantro

scallions

lamb   *Chinese rice wine*

sesame oil

light soy sauce

dark soy sauce

cilantro

garlic

brown sugar

1 Wrap the lamb and place in the freezer for about 1 hour, until just frozen. Cut the meat across the grain into paper-thin slices. Put the lamb slices in a bowl, add 2 tsp of the rice wine, the light soy sauce and ground Szechuan peppercorns. Mix well and allow to marinate for 15–30 minutes.

2 Make the sauce: in a bowl mix together the remaining rice wine, the salt, brown sugar, dark soy sauce and 2 tsp of the sesame oil. Set aside.

3 Heat a wok until hot, add the oil and swirl it around. Add the garlic and let it sizzle for a few seconds, then add the lamb. Stir-fry for about 1 minute, until the lamb is no longer pink. Pour in the sauce and stir briefly.

4 Add the scallions and cilantro and stir-fry for 15–20 seconds until the scallions just wilt. The finished dish should be slightly dry in appearance. Serve at once, sprinkled with the remaining sesame oil.

Veal Escalopes with Artichokes

Artichokes are very hard to prepare fresh, so use canned artichoke hearts, instead – they have an excellent flavor and are simple to use.

Serves 4

INGREDIENTS
1 lb veal escalopes
1 shallot
4 oz lean smoked bacon, finely
   chopped
1 × 14 oz can of artichoke hearts in
   brine, drained and quartered
⅔ cup veal stock
3 fresh rosemary sprigs
4 tbsp heavy cream
salt and freshly ground black pepper
fresh rosemary sprigs, to garnish

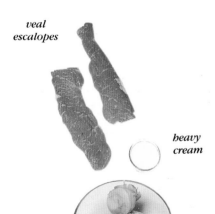

veal escalopes

heavy cream

artichoke hearts

1 Cut the veal into thin slices.

2 Using a sharp knife, cut the shallot into thin slices.

3 Heat the wok, then add the bacon. Stir-fry for 2 minutes. When the fat is released, add the veal and shallot and stir-fry for 3–4 minutes.

4 Add the artichokes and stir-fry for 1 minute. Stir in the stock and rosemary and simmer for 2 minutes. Stir in the heavy cream, season with salt and pepper and serve immediately, garnished with sprigs of fresh rosemary.

Indonesian-style Satay Chicken

Use boneless chicken thighs to give a good flavor to these satays.

Serves 4

INGREDIENTS

½ cup raw peanuts
3 tbsp vegetable oil
1 small onion, finely chopped
1 in piece ginger root, peeled and
   finely chopped
1 clove garlic, crushed
1½ lb chicken thighs, skinned and cut
   into cubes
3½ oz creamed coconut, chopped
1 tbsp chili sauce
4 tbsp chunky peanut butter
1 tsp soft dark brown sugar
⅔ cup milk
¼ tsp salt

COOK'S TIP

Soak bamboo skewers in cold water for at least 2 hours, or preferably overnight, so they do not char when keeping the threaded chicken warm in the oven.

1 Shell and rub the skins from the peanuts, then soak them in enough water to cover, for 1 minute. Drain the nuts and cut them into slivers.

2 Heat the wok and add 1 tsp oil. When the oil is hot, stir-fry the peanuts for 1 minute until crisp and golden. Remove with a slotted spoon and drain on paper towels.

3 Add the remaining oil to the hot wok. When the oil is hot, add the onion, ginger and garlic and stir-fry for 2–3 minutes until softened but not browned. Remove with a slotted spoon and drain on paper towels.

4 Add the chicken pieces and stir-fry for 3–4 minutes until crisp and golden on all sides. Thread on to pre-soaked bamboo skewers and keep warm.

5 Add the creamed coconut to the hot wok in small pieces and stir-fry until melted. Add the chili sauce, peanut butter and cooked ginger and garlic, and simmer for 2 minutes. Stir in the sugar, milk and salt, and simmer for a further 3 minutes. Serve the skewered chicken hot, with a dish of the hot dipping sauce sprinkled with the roasted peanuts.

creamed coconut

peanuts

chili sauce

peanut butter

Chili Beef with Basil

This is a dish for chili lovers! It is very easy to prepare and cook.

Serves 2

INGREDIENTS
about 6 tbsp peanut oil
16–20 large fresh basil leaves
10 oz round steak
2 tbsp Thai fish sauce
  (*nam pla*)
1 tsp dark brown sugar
1–2 fresh red chilies, sliced
  into rings
3 garlic cloves, chopped
1 tsp finely chopped
  fresh ginger
1 shallot, thinly sliced
2 tbsp finely chopped fresh
  basil leaves
squeeze of lemon juice
salt and ground black pepper
Thai jasmine rice, to serve

steak

shallot

Thai fish sauce

basil

garlic

sugar

ginger

peanut oil

red chili

1 Heat the oil in a wok and, when hot, add the basil leaves and fry for about 1 minute, until crisp and golden. Drain on paper towels. Remove the wok from the heat and pour off all but 2 tbsp of the oil.

2 Cut the steak across the grain into thin strips. In a bowl mix together the fish sauce and sugar. Add the beef, mix well, then allow to marinate for about 30 minutes.

3 Reheat the oil until hot, add the chili(es), garlic, ginger and shallot and stir-fry for 30 seconds. Add the beef and chopped basil, then stir-fry for about 3 minutes. Flavor with lemon juice and add seasoning to taste.

4 Transfer to a serving plate, sprinkle over the basil leaves and serve immediately with Thai jasmine rice.

Lemongrass Pork

Chilies and lemongrass flavor this simple stir-fry, while peanuts add crunch.

Serves 4

INGREDIENTS

1½ lb boneless pork loin
2 lemongrass stalks,
   finely chopped
4 scallions, thinly sliced
1 tsp salt
12 black peppercorns,
   coarsely crushed
2 tbsp peanut oil
2 garlic cloves, chopped
2 fresh red chilies, seeded
   and chopped
1 tsp light brown sugar
2 tbsp Thai fish sauce (*nam pla*),
   or to taste
¼ cup roasted unsalted peanuts,
   chopped
salt and ground black pepper
rice noodles, to serve
coarsely torn cilantro leaves,
   to garnish

scallions

red chilies

peanuts

pork

sugar

cilantro

lemongrass

garlic

Thai fish sauce

peanut oil

1 Trim any excess fat from the pork. Cut the meat across into ¼-in thick slices, then cut each slice into ¼-in strips. Put the pork into a bowl with the lemongrass, scallions, salt and crushed peppercorns; mix well. Cover and allow to marinate for 30 minutes.

2 Heat a wok until hot, add the oil and swirl it around. Add the pork mixture and stir-fry for 3 minutes.

3 Add the garlic and chilies and stir-fry for another 5–8 minutes over medium heat until the pork no longer looks pink.

4 Add the sugar, fish sauce and peanuts, and toss to mix. Taste and adjust the seasoning, if necessary. Serve at once on a bed of rice noodles, garnished with coarsely torn cilantro leaves.

Glazed Chicken with Cashew Nuts

Hoisin sauce lends a sweet yet slightly hot note to this chicken dish, while cashew nuts add a pleasing contrast of texture.

VARIATION
Use blanched almonds instead of cashew nuts if you prefer.

Serves 4

INGREDIENTS
¾ cup cashew nuts
1 red bell pepper
1 lb skinless and boneless
   chicken breasts
3 tbsp peanut oil
4 garlic cloves, finely chopped
2 tbsp Chinese rice wine or
   medium-dry sherry
3 tbsp hoisin sauce
2 tsp sesame oil
5–6 scallions,
   green parts only,
   cut into 1-in lengths

scallions

chicken

red pepper

cashew nuts

Chinese rice wine

garlic

peanut oil

hoisin sauce

sesame oil

1 Heat a wok until hot, add the cashew nuts and stir-fry over low to medium heat for 1–2 minutes, until golden brown. Remove and set aside.

2 Halve the pepper and remove the seeds. Slice the pepper and chicken into finger-length strips.

3 Heat the wok again until hot, add the oil and swirl it around. Add the garlic and let it sizzle in the oil for a few seconds. Add the pepper and chicken and stir-fry for 2 minutes.

4 Add the rice wine or sherry and hoisin sauce. Continue to stir-fry until the chicken is tender and all the ingredients are evenly glazed.

5 Stir in the sesame oil, toasted cashew nuts and scallion tips. Serve immediately with rice or noodles.

Spiced Lamb with Spinach

This recipe is based on *Sag Gosht* – meat cooked with spinach. The whole spices in this dish are not meant to be eaten.

Serves 3-4

INGREDIENTS

3 tbsp vegetable oil
1¼ lb lean boneless lamb,
   cut into 1-in cubes
1 onion, chopped
3 garlic cloves, finely chopped
½-in piece fresh ginger,
   finely chopped
6 black peppercorns
4 whole cloves
1 bay leaf
3 green cardamom pods, crushed
1 tsp ground cumin
1 tsp ground coriander
generous pinch of
   cayenne pepper
⅔ cup water
2 tomatoes, peeled, seeded
   and chopped
1 tsp salt
400 g/14 oz fresh spinach,
   trimmed, washed and
   finely chopped
1 tsp garam masala
crisp-fried onions and fresh
   cilantro sprigs, to garnish
nan bread or spiced basmati
   rice, to serve

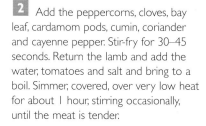

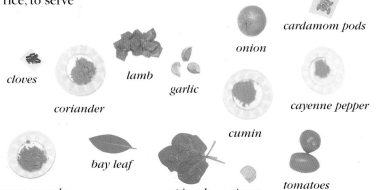

cloves   lamb   garlic   onion   cardamom pods
coriander   cayenne pepper
cumin
garam masala   bay leaf   spinach   ginger   tomatoes

1 Heat a kadhai or wok until hot. Add 2 tbsp of the oil and swirl it around. When hot, stir-fry the lamb in batches until evenly browned. Remove the lamb and set aside. Add the remaining oil, onion, garlic and ginger and stir-fry for 2–3 minutes.

2 Add the peppercorns, cloves, bay leaf, cardamom pods, cumin, coriander and cayenne pepper. Stir-fry for 30–45 seconds. Return the lamb and add the water, tomatoes and salt and bring to a boil. Simmer, covered, over very low heat for about 1 hour, stirring occasionally, until the meat is tender.

3 Increase the heat, then gradually add the spinach to the lamb, stirring to mix. Keep stirring and cooking until the spinach wilts completely and most, but not all of the liquid has evaporated and you are left with a thick green sauce. Stir in the garam masala. Garnish with crisp-fried onions and cilantro sprigs. Serve with nan bread or spiced basmati rice.

Duck and Ginger Chop Suey

Chicken can also be used in this recipe, but duck gives a richer contrast of flavors.

Serves 4

INGREDIENTS
2 duck breasts, about 6 oz each
3 tbsp sunflower oil
1 medium egg, lightly beaten
1 clove garlic
6 oz/2 cups bean sprouts
2 slices ginger root, cut into
  matchsticks
2 tsp oyster sauce
2 scallions, cut into matchsticks
salt and freshly ground pepper

FOR THE MARINADE
1 tbsp honey
2 tsp rice wine
2 tsp light soy sauce
2 tsp dark soy sauce

ginger

egg

bean sprouts

oyster sauce

duck breast

1 Remove the fat from the duck, cut the breasts into thin strips and place in a bowl. Mix the marinade ingredients together, pour over the duck, cover, chill and marinate overnight.

2 Next day, make the egg omelette. Heat a small frying pan and add 1 tbsp of the oil. When the oil is hot, pour in the egg and swirl around to make an omelet. Once cooked, leave it to cool and cut into strips. Drain the duck and discard the marinade.

3 Bruise the garlic with the flat blade of a knife. Heat the wok, then add 2 tsp oil. When the oil is hot, add the garlic and fry for 30 seconds, pressing it to release the flavor. Discard. Add the bean sprouts with seasoning and then stir-fry for about 30 seconds. Transfer to a heated dish, draining off any liquid.

4 Heat the wok and add the remaining oil. When the oil is hot, stir-fry the duck for 3 minutes until cooked. Add the ginger and oyster sauce and stir-fry for a further 2 minutes. Add the bean sprouts, egg strips and scallions, stir-fry briefly and serve immediately.

Chicken Tikka Masala

This recipe is based on *Makkhani Murghi*, a popular dish. Serve with warm nan bread or fluffy basmati rice.

Serves 4

INGREDIENTS
FOR THE MARINATED CHICKEN
4 chicken breasts,
    skinned
⅔ cup plain yogurt
1-in piece fresh ginger,
    finely grated
2 garlic cloves,
    crushed
1 tsp cayenne pepper
1 tbsp ground coriander
2 tbsp vegetable oil
2 tbsp lime juice
few drops each of yellow and
    red liquid food coloring,
    mixed to a bright orange shade

FOR THE MASALA
3 oz unsalted butter
1 tbsp vegetable oil
1 onion, chopped
1 lb tomatoes, peeled,
    seeded and chopped
1 tsp salt
1 fresh green chili, seeded and
    finely chopped
1 tsp garam masala
¼ tsp cayenne pepper
½ cup heavy cream
3 tbsp plain yogurt
2 tbsp fresh cilantro leaves,
    coarsely torn
1 tsp dry-roasted cumin
    seeds

COOK'S TIP
If you can, allow the chicken to marinate for as long as possible to allow plenty of time for it to absorb the flavorings.

1 Cut each chicken breast into three or four pieces, then slash the meaty side of each piece. Put the chicken into a shallow dish. In a bowl, mix together the yogurt, ginger, garlic, chili powder, ground coriander, oil, lime juice and coloring. Pour over the chicken and toss to coat completely, making sure that the marinade goes into the slits in the chicken. Cover and leave in the fridge for 6–24 hours, turning occasionally.

2 Preheat the oven to 450°F. Lift the chicken pieces out of the marinade, shaking off any excess liquid, and then arrange in a shallow baking tin. Bake for 15–20 minutes, until golden brown and cooked through.

cayenne pepper

chicken

cilantro

tomatoes

heavy cream

butter

cayenne pepper

ginger

green chili

food coloring

yogurt

vegetable oil

onion

coriander

3 Meanwhile, make the masala: heat the butter and oil in a kadhai or wok, add the onion and fry for 5 minutes, until softened. Add the tomatoes, salt, chili, garam masala and cayenne pepper. Cook, covered, for about 10 minutes.

4 Stir in the cream and yogurt, then simmer over low heat for 1–2 minutes, stirring constantly. Add the chicken pieces, then stir to coat in the sauce. Serve at once sprinkled with cilantro leaves and roasted cumin seeds.

Spiced Honey Chicken Wings

Be prepared to get very sticky when you eat these wings, as the best way to enjoy them is by eating them with your fingers. Provide individual finger bowls for your guests.

Serves 4

INGREDIENTS
1 red chili, finely chopped
1 tsp chili powder
1 tsp ground ginger
rind of 1 lime, finely grated
12 chicken wings
4 tbsp sunflower oil
1 tbsp fresh coriander, chopped
2 tbsp soy sauce
3½ tbsp honey
lime rind and fresh coriander sprigs,
   to garnish

lime

coriander

honey

chicken wing

1 Mix the fresh chili, chili powder, ground ginger and lime rind together. Rub the mixture into the chicken skins and leave for at least 2 hours to allow the flavors to penetrate.

2 Heat the wok and add half of the oil. When the oil is hot, add half the wings and stir-fry for 10 minutes, turning regularly until crisp and golden. Drain on paper towels. Repeat with the remaining wings.

4 Stir in the soy sauce and honey, and stir-fry for 1 minute. Serve the chicken wings hot with the sauce drizzled over them, garnished with lime rind and coriander sprigs.

3 Add the coriander to the hot wok and stir-fry for 30 seconds, then return the wings to the wok and stir-fry for about 1 minute.

Stir-fried Duck with Blueberries

Serve this conveniently quick dinner party dish with sprigs of fresh mint, which will give a wonderful fresh aroma as you bring the meal to the table.

Serves 4

INGREDIENTS
2 duck breasts, about 6 oz each
2 tbsp sunflower oil
1 tbsp red wine vinegar
1 tsp sugar
1 tsp red wine
1 tsp *crème de cassis* (black currant liqueur)
4 oz fresh blueberries
1 tbsp fresh mint, chopped
salt and freshly ground black pepper
fresh mint sprigs, to garnish
mixed green vegetables, steamed, to serve

duck

red wine vinegar

blueberries

red wine

mint

1 Cut the duck breasts into neat slices. Season well with salt and pepper.

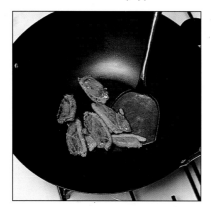

2 Heat the wok, then add the oil. When the oil is hot, stir-fry the duck for 3 minutes.

3 Add the red wine vinegar, sugar, red wine and *crème de cassis*. Bubble for 3 minutes, to reduce to a thick syrup.

4 Stir in the blueberries, sprinkle over the mint and serve garnished with sprigs of fresh mint.

Warm Stir-fried Salad

Warm salads are becoming increasingly popular because they are delicious and nutritious. Arrange the salad leaves on four individual plates, so the hot stir-fry can be served quickly on to them, ensuring the lettuce remains crisp and the chicken warm.

Serves 4

INGREDIENTS
1 tbsp fresh tarragon
2 boneless, skinless chicken breasts, about 8 oz each
2 in piece ginger root, peeled and finely chopped
3 tbsp light soy sauce
1 tbsp sugar
1 tbsp sunflower oil
1 Napa cabbage
½ chicory lettuce, torn into bite-size pieces
1 cup unsalted cashews
2 large carrots, peeled and cut into fine strips
salt and freshly ground black pepper

chicken breast

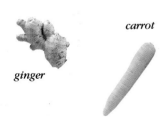

carrot

ginger

cashews

1 Chop the tarragon.

2 Cut the chicken into fine strips and place in a bowl.

3 To make the marinade, mix together in a bowl the tarragon, ginger, soy sauce, sugar and seasoning.

4 Pour the marinade over the chicken strips and leave for 2–4 hours.

5 Strain the chicken from the marinade. Heat the wok, then add the oil. When the oil is hot, stir-fry the chicken for 3 minutes, add the marinade and bubble for 2–3 minutes.

6 Slice the Napa cabbage and arrange on a plate with the chicory. Toss the cashews and carrots together with the chicken, pile on top of the bed of lettuce and serve immediately.

Sukiyaki-style Beef

This Japanese dish is a meal in itself; the recipe incorporates all the traditional elements – meat, vegetables, noodles and bean curd. If you want to do it all properly, eat the meal with chopsticks, and a spoon to collect the stock juices.

Serves 4

INGREDIENTS
1 lb thick rump steak
7 oz Japanese rice noodles
1 tbsp peanut oil
7 oz firm bean curd, cut
   into cubes
8 shiitake mushrooms, trimmed
2 medium leeks, sliced into 1 in
   lengths
3½ oz baby spinach, well washed,
   to serve

FOR THE STOCK
1 tbsp superfine sugar
6 tbsp rice wine
3 tbsp dark soy sauce
½ cup water

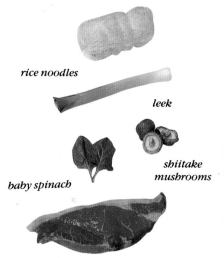

rice noodles

leek

baby spinach

shiitake mushrooms

rump steak

1 Cut the beef into thin slices.

2 Blanch the noodles in boiling water for 2 minutes. Strain well.

3 Mix together all the stock ingredients in a bowl.

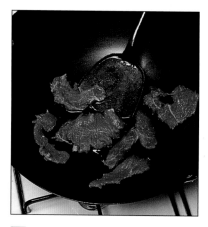

4 Heat the wok, then add the oil. When the oil is hot, stir-fry the beef for about 2–3 minutes, until it is cooked but still pink in color.

5 Pour the stock over the beef.

6 Add the remaining ingredients and cook for 4 minutes, until the leeks are tender. Serve a selection of the different ingredients, with a few baby spinach leaves, to each person.

Minted Lamb

Ask your butcher to remove the bone from a leg of lamb – it is sometimes called a butterflied leg of lamb – so that the meat can be sliced easily.

Serves 4

INGREDIENTS
1 lb boneless leg of lamb
2 tbsp fresh mint, chopped
½ lemon
1¼ cups natural low-fat yogurt
1 tbsp sunflower oil
salt and freshly ground black pepper
lemon wedges and fresh mint sprigs,
    to garnish

lemon

sunflower oil

mint

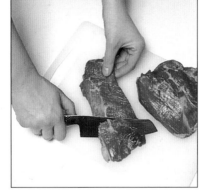

1 Using a sharp knife, cut the lamb into ¼-in thick slices. Place in a bowl.

2 Sprinkle half the mint over the lamb, season well with salt and pepper and leave for 20 minutes.

3 Roughly cut up the lemon and place in the food processor. Process until finely chopped. Empty it into a bowl, then stir in the yogurt and remaining mint.

4 Heat the wok, then add the oil. When the oil is hot, add the lamb and stir-fry for 4–5 minutes until cooked. Serve with the yogurt dressing, garnished with a lemon wedge and fresh mint sprigs.

Chicken Teriyaki

A bowl of boiled rice is the ideal accompaniment to this Japanese-style chicken dish.

Serves 4

INGREDIENTS
1 lb boneless, skinless chicken breasts

FOR THE MARINADE
1 tsp sugar
1 tbsp sake or rice wine
1 tbsp rice wine or dry sherry
2 tbsp dark soy sauce
rind of 1 orange, grated
orange segments and cress,
    to garnish

orange

rice wine

soy sauce

chicken breast

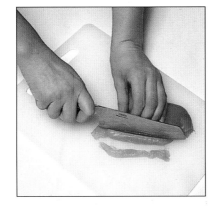

1 Finely slice the chicken.

2 Mix all the marinade ingredients together in a bowl.

COOK'S TIP

Make sure the marinade is brought to a boil and cooked for 4–5 minutes, because it has been in contact with raw chicken.

3 Place the chicken in a bowl, pour over the marinade and leave to marinate for 15 minutes.

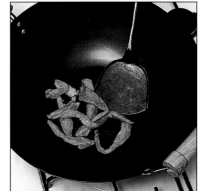

4 Heat the wok, add the chicken and marinade and stir-fry for 4–5 minutes. Serve garnished with orange segments and cress.

Stir-fried Turkey with Broccoli and Mushrooms

This is a really easy, tasty supper dish which works well with chicken too.

Serves 4

INGREDIENTS
4 oz broccoli florets
4 scallions
1 tsp cornstarch
3 tbsp oyster sauce
1 tbsp dark soy sauce
½ cup chicken stock,
   or bouillon cube
   and water
2 tsp lemon juice
3 tbsp peanut oil
1 lb turkey fillets, cut into
   strips, about ¼ x 2 in
1 small onion, chopped
2 garlic cloves, crushed
2 tsp fresh ginger,
   finely grated
4 oz fresh shiitake
   mushrooms, sliced
3 oz canned baby corn,
   halved lengthwise
1 tbsp sesame oil
salt and ground black pepper
egg noodles, to serve

broccoli

scallion

onion

oyster sauce   *turkey*   *mushrooms*

lemon

dark soy sauce

peanut oil

baby corn   *garlic*

chicken stock

1 Divide the broccoli florets into smaller sprigs and cut the stalks into thin diagonal slices.

2 Finely chop the white parts of the scallions and slice the green parts into thin shreds.

3 In a bowl, blend together the cornstarch, oyster sauce, soy sauce, stock and lemon juice. Set aside.

4 Heat a wok until hot, add 2 tbsp of the peanut oil and swirl it around. Add the turkey and stir-fry for about 2 minutes, until golden and crispy at the edges. Remove the turkey from the wok and keep warm.

5 Add the remaining peanut oil to the wok and stir-fry the chopped onion, garlic and ginger over medium heat for about 1 minute. Increase the heat to high, add the broccoli, mushrooms and corn and stir-fry for 2 minutes.

6 Return the turkey to the wok, then add the sauce with the chopped scallion and seasoning. Cook, stirring, for about 1 minute, until the sauce has thickened. Then stir in the sesame oil. Serve immediately on a bed of egg noodles with the finely shredded scallion sprinkled on top.

Thai Red Chicken Curry

Here chicken and potatoes are simmered in spiced coconut milk, then garnished with shredded kaffir lime leaves and red chilies.

Serves 4

INGREDIENTS
1 onion
1 tbsp peanut oil
1⅔ cups coconut milk
2 tbsp red curry paste
2 tbsp Thai fish sauce
  (*nam pla*)
1 tbsp light brown sugar
8 oz tiny new potatoes
1 lb skinless chicken breasts,
  cut into chunks
1 tbsp lime juice
2 tbsp fresh mint,
  finely chopped
1 tbsp fresh basil,
  finely chopped
2 kaffir lime leaves, shredded
1–2 fresh red chilies, seeded and
  finely shredded
salt and ground black pepper

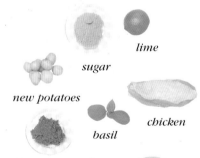

lime

sugar

new potatoes

chicken

basil

red curry paste

onion

coconut milk

mint

Thai fish sauce

You can use boneless chicken thighs instead of breasts. Simply skin them, cut the flesh into chunks and cook in the coconut milk with the potatoes.

1 Cut the onion into wedges.

2 Heat a wok until hot, add the oil and swirl it around. Add the onion and stir-fry for 3–4 minutes.

3 Pour in the coconut milk, then bring to a boil, stirring. Stir in the curry paste, fish sauce and sugar.

4 Add the potatoes and seasoning and simmer gently, covered, for about 20 minutes.

5 Add the chicken chunks and cook, covered, over low heat for another 5–10 minutes, until the chicken and potatoes are tender.

6 Stir in the lime juice, chopped mint and basil. Serve at once, sprinkled with the shredded kaffir lime leaves and red chilies.

Stir-fried Pork with Lychees

Lychees have a very pretty pink skin which, when peeled, reveals a soft fleshy berry with a hard shiny pit. If you cannot buy fresh lychees, this dish can be made with drained canned lychees.

Serves 4

INGREDIENTS
1 lb fatty pork, for example belly pork
2 tbsp hoisin sauce
4 scallions, sliced
6 oz lychees, peeled, pitted and cut
    into slivers
salt and freshly ground pepper
fresh lychees and fresh parsley sprigs,
    to garnish

pork

hoisin sauce

scallions

lychees

1 Cut the pork into bite-size pieces.

2 Pour the hoisin sauce over the pork and marinate for 30 minutes.

3 Heat the wok, then add the pork and stir-fry for 5 minutes until crisp and golden. Add the scallions and stir-fry for a further 2 minutes.

4 Scatter the lychee slivers over the pork, and season well with salt and pepper. Garnish with fresh lychees and fresh parsley, and serve.

Oriental Beef

This sumptuously rich beef melts in the mouth, and is perfectly complemented by the cool, crunchy relish.

Serves 4

INGREDIENTS
1 lb rump steak

FOR THE MARINADE
1 tbsp sunflower oil
2 cloves garlic, crushed
4 tbsp dark soy sauce
2 tbsp dry sherry
2 tsp soft dark brown sugar

FOR THE RELISH
6 radishes
4 in piece cucumber
1 piece preserved ginger
4 whole radishes, to garnish

rump steak

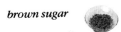

brown sugar

soy sauce

garlic

radish

1 Cut the beef into thin strips. Place in a bowl.

2 To make the marinade, mix together the garlic, soy sauce, sherry and sugar in a bowl. Pour it over the beef and leave to marinate overnight.

3 To make the relish, chop the radishes and cucumber into matchsticks and the ginger into small matchsticks. Mix well together in a bowl.

4 Heat the wok, then add the oil. When the oil is hot, add the meat and marinade and stir-fry for 3–4 minutes. Serve with the relish, and garnish with a whole radish on each plate.

Sweet-sour Duck with Mango

Mango adds natural sweetness to this colorful stir-fry. Crispy deep-fried noodles make the perfect accompaniment.

Serves 4

INGREDIENTS
8–12 oz duck breasts
3 tbsp dark soy sauce
1 tbsp Chinese rice wine
1 tsp sesame oil
1 tsp Chinese five-
    spice powder
1 tbsp brown sugar
2 tsp cornstarch
3 tbsp Chinese rice vinegar
1 tbsp tomato ketchup
1 mango, not too ripe
3 baby eggplant
1 red onion
1 carrot
4 tbsp peanut oil
1 garlic clove, sliced
1-in piece fresh ginger,
    cut into shreds
3 oz sugar snap peas

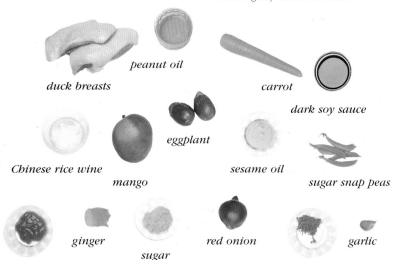

duck breasts

peanut oil

carrot

dark soy sauce

eggplant

Chinese rice wine

mango

sesame oil

sugar snap peas

ginger

sugar

red onion

garlic

tomato ketchup

Chinese five-spice powder

1 Thinly slice the duck breasts and place in a bowl. Mix together 1 tbsp of the soy sauce with the rice wine or sherry, sesame oil and five-spice powder. Pour over the duck, cover and allow to marinate for 1–2 hours. In a separate bowl, blend together the sugar, cornstarch, rice vinegar, ketchup and remaining soy sauce. Set aside.

2 Peel the mango, slice the flesh from the pit, then cut into thick strips. Slice the eggplant, onion and carrot into similar-sized pieces.

3 Heat a wok until hot, add 2 tbsp of the oil and swirl it around. Drain the duck, reserving the marinade. Stir-fry the duck slices over high heat until the fat is crisp and golden. Remove and keep warm. Add 1 tbsp of the oil to the wok and stir-fry the eggplant for 3 minutes until golden.

4 Add the remaining oil and fry the onion, garlic, ginger and carrot for 2–3 minutes, then add the sugar snap peas and stir-fry for another 2 minutes.

5 Add the mango and return the duck with the sauce and reserved marinade to the wok. Cook, stirring, until the sauce thickens slightly. Serve at once.

Stir-fried Pork with Mustard

Fry the apples for this dish very carefully, because they will disintegrate if they are overcooked.

Serves 4

INGREDIENTS

1¼ lb pork fillet
1 tart apple, such as Granny Smith
3 tbsp unsalted butter
1 tbsp superfine sugar
1 small onion, finely chopped
2 tbsp Calvados, Applejack or
    other brandy
1 tbsp Meaux or coarse-grain
    mustard
⅔ cup heavy cream
2 tbsp fresh parsley, chopped
salt and freshly ground black pepper
flat-leaf parsley sprigs, to garnish

pork fillet

onion

mustard

apple

1 Cut the pork fillet into thin slices.

2 Peel and core the apple. Cut it into thick slices.

3 Heat the wok, then add half the butter. When the butter is hot, add the apple slices, sprinkle over the sugar, and stir-fry for 2–3 minutes. Remove the apple and set aside. Wipe out the wok with paper towels.

4 Heat the wok, then add the remaining butter and stir-fry the pork fillet and onion together for 2–3 minutes, until the pork is golden and the onion has begun to soften.

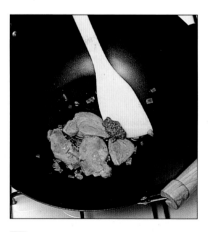

5 Stir in the Calvados, Applejack or other brandy and boil until it is reduced by half. Stir in the mustard.

6 Add the cream and simmer for 1 minute, then stir in the parsley. Serve garnished with sprigs of flat-leaf parsley.

Buffalo-Style Chicken Wings

This fiery-hot fried chicken recipe is said to have originated in the town of Buffalo, New York, but is now popular everywhere. Serve it with traditional Blue-cheese Dip and celery sticks.

Makes 48

INGREDIENTS

24 plump chicken wings, tips
   removed
vegetable oil for frying
salt
6 tablespoons butter
¼ cup hot-pepper sauce, or to taste
1 tablespoon white or cider vinegar
celery sticks, to serve

FOR THE BLUE-CHEESE DIP

4 ounces blue cheese, such as Danish
   blue
½ cup mayonnaise
½ cup sour cream
2 to 3 green onions, finely chopped
1 garlic clove, finely chopped
1 tablespoon white or cider vinegar

1 To make the dip, use a fork to gently mash the blue cheese against the side of a bowl. Add the mayonnaise, sour cream, green onions, garlic, and vinegar and stir together until well blended. Refrigerate until ready to serve.

green onions

Danish blue cheese

sour cream

vegetable oil

white vinegar

chicken wings

mayonnaise

butter

hot-pepper sauce

2 Using kitchen scissors or a sharp knife, cut each wing in half at the joint to make 48 pieces in all.

3 In a large saucepan or wok, heat 2 inches of oil until hot but not smoking. Fry the chicken wing pieces in small batches for 8 to 10 minutes until crisp and golden, turning once. Drain on paper towels. Season and arrange in a bowl.

4 In a small saucepan over medium-low heat, melt the butter. Stir in the hot-pepper sauce and vinegar and immediately pour over the chicken, tossing to combine. Serve hot with the blue-cheese dip and celery sticks.

Cellophane Noodles with Pork

Unlike other types of noodle, cellophane noodles can be successfully reheated.

Serves 3-4

INGREDIENTS
4 oz cellophane noodles
4 dried Chinese black
   mushrooms
8 oz boneless lean pork
2 tbsp dark soy sauce
2 tbsp Chinese rice wine
2 garlic cloves, crushed
1 tbsp fresh ginger
   finely grated
1 tsp chili oil
3 tbsp peanut oil
4-6 scallions, chopped
1 tsp cornstarch blended with
   ¾ cup chicken stock or water
2 tbsp cilantro,
   finely chopped
salt and ground black pepper
cilantro sprigs, to garnish

scallions

noodles

chicken stock   Chinese rice wine

mushrooms

dark soy sauce

pork

chili oil   peanut oil

1 Put the noodles and mushrooms in separate bowls and pour over warm water to cover. Let soak for 15–20 minutes until soft; drain well. Cut the noodles into 5 in lengths, using scissors or a knife. Squeeze out any water from the mushrooms, discard the stems and then finely chop the caps.

2 Meanwhile, cut the pork into very small cubes. Put into a bowl with the soy sauce, rice wine, garlic, ginger and chili oil, then let stand for about 15 minutes. Drain, reserving the marinade.

3 Heat a wok until hot, add the oil and swirl it around. Add the pork and mushrooms and stir-fry for 3 minutes. Add the scallions and stir-fry for 1 minute. Stir in the cornstarch, marinade and seasoning. Cook for about 1 minute.

4 Add the noodles and stir-fry for about 2 minutes, until the noodles absorb most of the liquid and the pork is cooked through. Stir in the chopped cilantro. Taste and adjust the seasoning. Serve garnished with cilantro sprigs.

Sizzling Beef with Celeriac Straw

The crisp celeriac matchsticks look like fine pieces of straw when cooked and have a mild celery-like flavor that is quite delicious.

Serves 4

INGREDIENTS
1 lb celeriac
⅔ cup vegetable oil
1 red pepper
6 scallions
1 lb rump steak
4 tbsp beef stock
2 tbsp sherry vinegar
2 tsp Worcestershire sauce
2 tsp tomato paste
salt and freshly ground black pepper

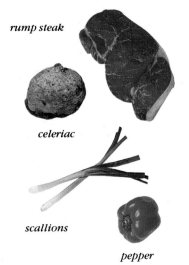

rump steak

celeriac

scallions

pepper

1 Peel the celeriac and then cut it into fine matchsticks, using a cleaver.

2 Heat the wok, then add two-thirds of the oil. When the oil is hot, fry the celeriac matchsticks in batches until golden brown and crispy. Drain well on paper towels.

3 Chop the red pepper and the scallions into approximate 1 in lengths, using diagonal cuts.

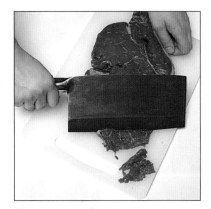

4 Chop the beef into strips, across the grain of the meat.

5 Heat the wok, and then add the remaining oil. When the oil is hot, stir-fry the chopped scallions and red pepper for 2–3 minutes.

6 Add the beef strips and stir-fry for a further 3–4 minutes until well browned. Add the stock, vinegar, Worcestershire sauce and tomato paste. Season well and serve with the celeriac straw.

Turkey with Sage, Prunes and Brandy

This stir-fry has a very rich sauce based on a good brandy – use the best you can afford.

Serves 4

INGREDIENTS
4 oz prunes
3–3½ lb turkey breast
1¼ cups VSOP cognac or
    good brandy
1 tbsp fresh sage, chopped
5 oz smoked bacon, in one piece
4 tbsp butter
24 pearl onions, peeled and quartered
salt and freshly ground black pepper
fresh sage sprigs, to garnish

smoked bacon

prunes

pearl onion

sage

1 Pit the prunes and cut them into slivers. Remove the skin from the turkey and cut the breast into thin pieces.

2 Mix together the prunes, turkey, cognac and sage in a non-metallic dish. Cover and leave to marinate overnight.

3 Next day, strain the turkey and prunes, reserving the cognac mixture, and pat dry on paper towels.

4 Cut the bacon into lardons (dice).

5 Heat the wok and add half the butter. When melted, add the onions and stir-fry for 4 minutes until crisp and golden. Set aside.

6 Heat the wok, add the lardons and stir-fry for 1 minute until the bacon begins to release some fat. Add the remaining butter and stir-fry the turkey and prunes for 3–4 minutes until crisp and golden. Push the turkey mixture to one side in the wok, add the cognac and simmer until thickened. Stir the turkey into the sauce, season well with salt and ground black pepper, and serve garnished with sage.

Glazed Lamb

Lemon and honey make a classically good combination in sweet dishes, and this lamb recipe shows how well they work together in savory dishes, too. Serve with a fresh mixed salad to complete this delicious dish.

Serves 4

INGREDIENTS
1 lb boneless lean lamb
1 tbsp grapeseed oil
6 oz mange tout peas, topped
    and tailed
3 scallions, sliced
2 tbsp honey
juice of half a lemon
2 tbsp fresh coriander, chopped
1 tbsp sesame seeds
salt and freshly ground pepper

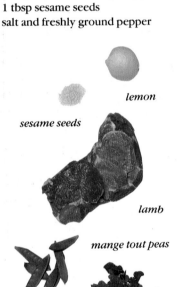

lemon

sesame seeds

lamb

mange tout peas

coriander

1 Using a sharp knife, cut the lamb into thin strips.

2 Heat the wok, then add the oil. When the oil is hot, stir-fry the lamb until browned all over. Remove from the wok and keep warm.

3 Add the mange tout peas and scallions to the hot wok and stir-fry for 30 seconds.

4 Return the lamb to the wok and add the honey, lemon juice, coriander and sesame seeds, and season well. Bring to a boil and bubble for 1 minute until the lamb is well coated in the honey mixture.

Spicy Beef

Promoting a fast-growing trend in worldwide cuisine, the wok is used in this recipe to produce a colorful and healthy meal.

Serves 4

INGREDIENTS
1 tbsp oil
1 lb/4 cups ground beef
1 in fresh ginger root, sliced
1 tsp Chinese five-spice powder
1 red chili, sliced
2 oz snow peas
1 red bell pepper, chopped
1 carrot, sliced
4 oz beansprouts
1 tbsp sesame oil

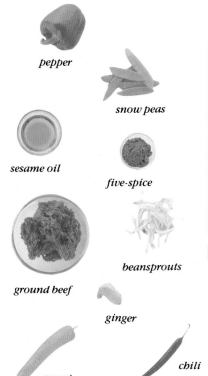

pepper

snow peas

sesame oil

five-spice

beansprouts

ground beef

ginger

carrot

chili

1 Heat the oil in a wok until almost smoking. Add the ground beef and cook for 3 minutes, stirring all the time.

2 Add the ginger, Chinese five-spice powder and chili. Cook for 1 minute.

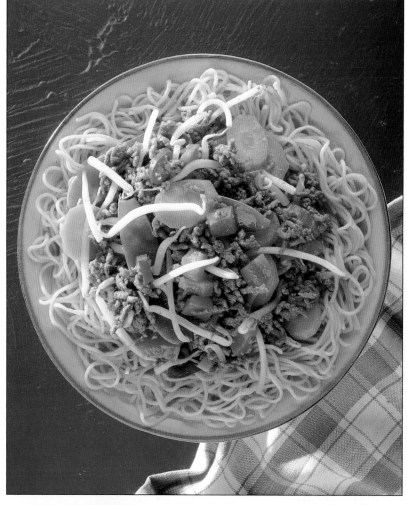

3 Add the snow peas, pepper and carrot and cook for a further 3 minutes, stirring continuously.

4 Add the beansprouts and sesame oil and cook for a final 2 minutes. Serve immediately with noodles.

Stir-fried Sweet and Sour Chicken

There are few cooking concepts that are better suited to today's busy lifestyle than the all-in-one stir-fry. This one has a South-east Asian influence.

Serves 4

INGREDIENTS
10 oz Chinese egg noodles
2 tbsp vegetable oil
3 scallions, chopped
1 garlic clove, crushed
1 in fresh ginger root, peeled and
    grated
1 tsp hot paprika
1 tsp ground coriander
3 boneless chicken breasts, sliced
1 cup sugar-snap peas, topped
    and tailed
4 oz baby corn, halved
8 oz fresh bean sprouts
1 tbsp cornstarch
3 tbsp soy sauce
3 tbsp lemon juice
1 tbsp sugar
3 tbsp chopped fresh cilantro or
    scallion tops, to garnish

COOK'S TIP

Large wok lids are cumbersome and can be difficult to store in a small kitchen. Consider placing a circle of waxed paper against the food surface to keep cooking juices in.

1 Bring a large saucepan of salted water to a boil. Add the noodles and cook according to the package instructions. Drain, cover and keep warm.

2 Heat the oil. Add the scallions and cook over a gentle heat. Mix in the next five ingredients, then stir-fry for 3–4 minutes. Add the next three ingredients and steam briefly. Add the noodles.

3 Combine the cornstarch, soy sauce, lemon juice and sugar in a small bowl. Add to the wok and simmer briefly to thicken. Serve garnished with chopped cilantro or scallion tops.

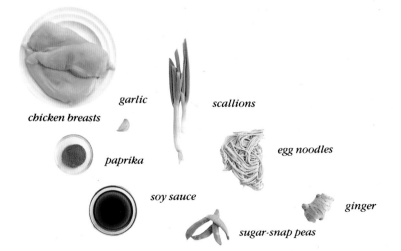

chicken breasts
garlic
scallions
paprika
egg noodles
soy sauce
ginger
sugar-snap peas

Stir-fried Beef and Broccoli

This spicy beef may be served with noodles or on a bed of boiled rice for a speedy and low calorie Chinese meal.

Serves 4

INGREDIENTS

12 oz sirloin or lean London broil steak
1 tbsp cornstarch
1 tsp sesame oil
12 oz broccoli, cut into small florets
4 scallions, sliced on the diagonal
1 carrot, cut into matchstick strips
1 garlic clove, crushed
1 in piece ginger root, cut into very fine strips
½ cup low fat beef stock
2 tbsp soy sauce
2 tbsp dry sherry
2 tsp light brown sugar
scallion tassels, to garnish
noodles or rice, to serve

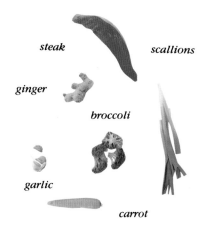

steak
scallions
ginger
broccoli
garlic
carrot

1 Trim the beef and cut into thin slices across the grain. Cut each slice into thin strips. Toss in the cornstarch to coat thoroughly.

2 Heat the sesame oil in a large non-stick frying pan or wok. Add the beef strips and stir-fry over a brisk heat for 3 minutes. Remove and set aside.

COOK'S TIP

To make scallion tassels, trim the bulb base then cut the green shoot so that the onion is 3 in long. Shred to within 1 in of the base and put into iced water for 1 hour.

3 Add the broccoli, scallions, carrot, garlic clove, ginger and stock to the frying pan or wok. Cover and simmer for 3 minutes. Uncover and cook, stirring until all the stock has reduced entirely.

4 Mix the soy sauce, sherry and brown sugar together. Add to the frying pan or wok with the beef. Cook for 2–3 minutes stirring continuously. Spoon into a warm serving dish and garnish with scallion tassels. Serve on a bed of noodles or rice.

Stir-fried Parsnips

Serve these sweet and piquant parsnips as an accompaniment to roast beef or as a vegetarian starter for two.

Serves 4 as an accompaniment

INGREDIENTS
2 large cloves garlic
12 oz parsnips
1 tbsp vegetable oil
1 in piece ginger root, peeled
   and grated
rind of 1 lime, grated
3 tbsp honey
salt and freshly ground black pepper

lime

ginger

garlic

parsnip

1 Peel and cut the garlic into slices.

2 Peel and cut the parsnips into long, thin strands.

3 Heat the wok, then swirl in the oil. When the oil is hot, stir-fry the parsnips for 2 minutes.

4 Sprinkle the ginger, lime rind, salt and pepper and honey over the parsnips. Stir to coat the vegetables and serve.

Stir-fried Spinach with Garlic and Sesame Seeds

The sesame seeds add a crunchy texture which contrasts well with the wilted spinach in this easy vegetable dish.

Serves 2

INGREDIENTS
8 oz fresh spinach, washed
1½ tbsp sesame seeds
2 tbsp peanut oil
¼ tsp sea salt flakes
2–3 garlic cloves, sliced

spinach

peanut oil

garlic

sesame seeds

1 Shake the spinach to get rid of any excess water, then remove the stalks and discard any yellow or damaged leaves. Lay several spinach leaves one on top of another, roll up tightly and cut crossways into wide strips. Repeat with the remaining leaves.

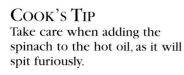

COOK'S TIP
Take care when adding the spinach to the hot oil, as it will spit furiously.

2 Heat a wok to medium heat, add the sesame seeds and dry-fry, stirring, for 1–2 minutes, until golden brown. Transfer to a small bowl and set aside.

3 Add the oil to the wok and swirl it around. When hot, add the salt, spinach and garlic and stir-fry for 2 minutes until the spinach just wilts and the leaves are coated with the oil.

4 Sprinkle over the sesame seeds and toss well. Serve at once.

Stir-fried Vegetables with Cilantro Omelet

This is a great supper dish for vegetarians. The glaze is added here only to make the mixture shine, it is not intended as a sauce.

Serves 3-4

INGREDIENTS
FOR THE OMELET
2 eggs
2 tbsp water
3 tbsp chopped cilantro
salt and ground black pepper
1 tbsp peanut oil

FOR THE GLAZED VEGETABLES
1 tbsp cornstarch
2 tbsp dry sherry
1 tbsp sweet chili sauce
½ cup vegetable stock, or
   vegetable bouillon cube
   and water
2 tbsp peanut oil
1 tsp fresh ginger,
   finely grated
6–8 scallions, sliced
4 oz snow peas
1 yellow bell pepper,
   seeded and sliced
4 oz fresh shiitake or
   button mushrooms
3 oz (drained weight)
   canned water chestnuts, rinsed
4 oz beansprouts
½ small Chinese cabbage,
   coarsely shredded

egg

cilantro

snow peas

peanut oil

scallion

mushrooms

yellow pepper

stock

sweet chili sauce

Chinese cabbage

beansprouts

1 Make the omelet: whisk the eggs, water, cilantro and seasoning in a small bowl. Heat the oil in a wok. Pour in the eggs, then tilt the wok so that the mixture spreads to an even layer. Cook over high heat until the edges are slightly crisp.

2 With a wok or spatula, flip the omelet over and cook the other side for about 30 seconds, until lightly browned. Turn the omelet onto a board and allow to cool. When cold, roll up loosely and cut into thin slices. Wipe the wok clean.

3 In a bowl, blend together the cornstarch, soy sauce, chili sauce and stock. Set aside.

4 Heat the wok until hot, add the oil and swirl it around, add the ginger and scallions and stir-fry for a few seconds to flavor the oil. Add the snow peas, pepper, mushrooms and water chestnuts and stir-fry for 3 minutes.

VARIATION

Vary the combination of vegetables used according to availability and taste.

5 Add the beansprouts and Chinese cabbage and stir-fry for 2 minutes.

6 Pour in the glaze ingredients and cook, stirring, for about 1 minute until the glaze thickens and coats the vegetables. Turn the vegetables onto a warmed serving plate and top with the omelet shreds. Serve at once.

Crispy Cabbage

This makes a wonderful accompaniment to meat or vegetable dishes – just a couple of spoonfuls will add crispy texture to a meal. It goes especially well with shrimp dishes.

Serves 2–4 as an accompaniment

INGREDIENTS
4 juniper berries
1 large Savoy cabbage
4 tbsp vegetable oil
1 clove garlic, crushed
1 tsp superfine sugar
1 tsp salt

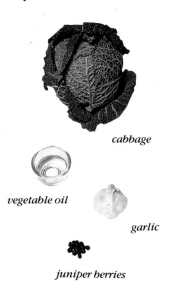

cabbage

vegetable oil

garlic

juniper berries

1 Finely crush the juniper berries, using a pestle and mortar.

2 Finely shred the cabbage.

3 Heat the wok, then add the oil. When the oil is hot, stir-fry the garlic for 1 minute. Add the cabbage and stir-fry for 3–4 minutes until crispy. Remove and pat dry with paper towels.

4 Return the cabbage to the wok. Toss the cabbage in sugar, salt and crushed juniper berries and serve hot or cold.

Szechuan Eggplant

This dish is also known as fish-fragrant eggplant, as the eggplant is cooked with flavorings that are often used with fish.

Serves 4

INGREDIENTS
2 small eggplant
1 tsp salt
3 dried red chilies
peanut oil, for deep frying
3–4 garlic cloves, finely chopped
½-in piece fresh ginger, finely chopped
4 scallions, cut into 1-in lengths (white and green parts separated)
1 tbsp Chinese rice wine or medium-dry sherry
1 tbsp light soy sauce
1 tsp sugar
¼ tsp ground roasted Szechuan peppercorns
1 tbsp Chinese rice vinegar
1 tsp sesame oil

ginger

eggplant

dried red chilies

scallions

Chinese rice wine

light soy sauce

sesame oil

garlic

peanut oil

1 Trim the eggplant and cut into strips, about 1½ in wide and 3 in long. Place the eggplant in a colander and sprinkle over the salt. Set aside for 30 minutes, then rinse them thoroughly under cold running water. Pat dry with paper towels.

2 Meanwhile, soak the chilies in warm water for 15 minutes. Drain, then cut each chili into three or four pieces, discarding the seeds.

3 Half-fill a wok with oil and heat to 350°F. Deep-fry the eggplant, until golden brown. Drain on paper towels. Pour off most of the oil from the wok. Reheat the oil and add the garlic, ginger and white scallion.

4 Stir-fry for 30 seconds. Add the eggplant and toss, then add the rice wine or sherry, soy sauce, sugar, ground Szechuan peppercorns and rice vinegar. Stir-fry for 1–2 minutes. Sprinkle over the sesame oil and green scallion.

Spiced Vegetables with Coconut

This spicy and substantial dish could be served as a starter, or as a vegetarian main course for two. Eat it with spoons and forks, and hunks of granary bread for mopping up the delicious coconut milk.

Serves 2–4 as a starter

INGREDIENTS
1 red chili
2 large carrots
6 stalks celery
1 bulb fennel
2 tbsp grapeseed oil
1 in piece ginger root, peeled
   and grated
1 clove garlic, crushed
3 scallions, sliced
1 × 14 fl oz can thin coconut milk
1 tbsp fresh coriander, chopped
salt and freshly ground black pepper
coriander sprigs, to garnish

celery

scallions

fennel

carrot

1 Halve, deseed and finely chop the chili. If necessary, wear rubber gloves to protect your hands.

2 Slice the carrots on the diagonal. Slice the celery stalks on the diagonal.

3 Trim the fennel head and slice roughly, using a sharp knife.

4 Heat the wok, then add the oil. When the oil is hot, add the ginger and garlic, chili, carrots, celery, fennel and scallions and stir-fry for 2 minutes.

5 Stir in the coconut milk with a large spoon and bring to a boil.

6 Stir in the coriander and salt and pepper, and serve garnished with coriander sprigs.

Chinese Greens with Oyster Sauce

Here Chinese greens are prepared in a very simple way – stir-fried and served with oyster sauce. The combination makes a simple, quickly prepared, tasty accompaniment.

Serves 3-4

INGREDIENTS
1 lb Chinese greens
  (*bok choy*)
2 tbsp peanut oil
1–2 tbsp oyster sauce

Chinese greens

peanut oil

oyster sauce

VARIATION
You can replace the Chinese greens with Chinese flowering cabbage, or Chinese broccoli, which is also known by its Cantonese name *choi sam*. It has green leaves and tiny yellow flowers, which are also eaten along with the leaves and stalks. It is available at Asian markets.

1 Trim the Chinese greens, removing any discolored leaves and damaged stems. Tear into manageable pieces.

2 Heat a wok until hot, add the oil and swirl it around.

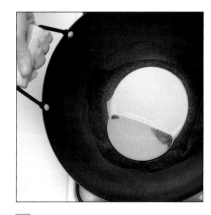

3 Add the Chinese greens and stir-fry for 2–3 minutes, until the greens have wilted a little.

4 Add the oyster sauce and continue to stir-fry a few seconds more until the greens are cooked but still slightly crisp. Serve immediately.

Deep-fried Root Vegetables with Spiced Salt

All kinds of root vegetables may be finely sliced and deep-fried to make "chips". Serve as an accompaniment to an oriental-style meal or simply by themselves as a nibble.

Serves 4-6

INGREDIENTS
1 carrot
2 parsnips
2 raw beets
1 sweet potato
peanut oil, for deep frying
¼ tsp cayenne pepper
1 tsp sea salt flakes

cayenne pepper

sweet potato

peanut oil

beet

carrot

parsnips

1 Peel all the vegetables, then slice the carrot and parsnips into long, thin ribbons, and the beets and sweet potato into thin rounds. Pat dry all the vegetables on paper towels.

COOK'S TIP

To save time, you can slice the vegetables using a mandoline or a blender or food processor with a thin slicing disc attached.

2 Half-fill a wok with oil and heat to 350°F. Add the vegetable slices in batches and deep-fry for 2–3 minutes, until golden and crisp. Remove and drain on paper towels.

3 Place the cayenne pepper and sea salt in a mortar and grind together to a coarse powder.

4 Pile up the vegetable "chips" on a serving plate and sprinkle over the spiced salt.

Yellow Flower Vegetables

To serve, each person spreads hoisin sauce on a pancake, adds filling and rolls it up.

Serves 4

INGREDIENTS

3 eggs
2 tbsp water
4 tbsp peanut oil
1 oz dried Chinese black
  mushrooms
1 oz dried wood ears
2 tsp cornstarch
2 tbsp light soy sauce
2 tbsp Chinese rice wine or
  medium-dry sherry
2 tsp sesame oil
2 garlic cloves, finely chopped
½-in piece fresh ginger,
  cut into thin shreds
3 oz canned sliced bamboo
  shoots (drained weight), rinsed
6 oz beansprouts
4 scallions, finely shredded
salt and ground black pepper
Chinese pancakes and hoisin
  sauce, to serve

COOK'S TIP
Chinese pancakes are available at Asian markets. Reheat them in a bamboo steamer for 2–3 minutes before serving.

1 Whisk the eggs, water and seasoning in a small bowl. Heat 1 tbsp of the peanut oil in a wok and swirl it around. Pour in the eggs, then tilt the wok so that they spread to an even layer. Continue to cook over high heat for about 2 minutes, until set. Turn onto a board and, when cool, roll up and cut into thin strips. Wipe the wok clean.

2 Meanwhile, put the black mushrooms and wood ears into separate bowls. Pour over enough warm water to cover, then allow to soak for 20–30 minutes, until soft. Drain the dried mushrooms, reserving their soaking liquid. Squeeze the excess liquid from each of them.

3 Remove the tough stalks and thinly slice the black mushrooms. Finely shred the wood ears. Set aside. Strain the reserved soaking liquid through muslin into a measuring cup; reserve ½ cup of the liquid. Then, in a bowl, blend the cornstarch with the reserved liquid, soy sauce, rice wine or sherry and sesame oil.

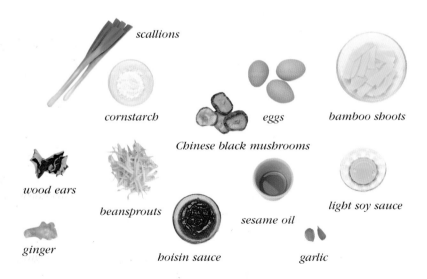

scallions

cornstarch

Chinese black mushrooms

eggs

bamboo shoots

wood ears

beansprouts

sesame oil

light soy sauce

ginger

hoisin sauce

garlic

4 Heat the wok over medium heat, add the remaining peanut oil and swirl it around. Add the wood ears and black mushrooms and stir-fry for about 2 minutes. Add the garlic, ginger, bamboo shoots and beansprouts and stir-fry for 1–2 minutes.

5 Pour in the cornstarch mixture and cook, stirring, for 1 minute until thickened. Add the scallions and omelet strips and toss gently. Adjust the seasoning, adding more soy sauce, if needed. Serve at once with the Chinese pancakes and hoisin sauce.

Spicy Vegetable Fritters with Thai Salsa

The Thai salsa goes just as well with plain stir-fried salmon strips or stir-fried beef as it does with these zucchini fritters.

Serves 2–4 as a starter

INGREDIENTS
2 tsp cumin seeds
2 tsp coriander seeds
1 lb zucchini
1 cup chickpea (gram) flour
½ tsp baking soda
½ cup peanut oil
fresh mint sprigs, to garnish

FOR THE THAI SALSA
½ cucumber, diced
3 scallions, chopped
6 radishes, cubed
2 tbsp fresh mint, chopped
1 in piece ginger root, peeled and grated
3 tbsp lime juice
2 tbsp superfine sugar
3 cloves garlic, crushed

cucumber

mint   *ginger*

radishes

zucchini

1 Heat the wok, then toast the cumin and coriander seeds. Cool them, then grind well, using a pestle and mortar.

2 Cut the zucchini into 3 in sticks. Place in a bowl.

3 Blend the flour, baking soda, spices and salt and pepper in a food processor. Add ¼ cup warm water with 1 tbsp peanut oil, and blend again.

4 Coat the zucchini in the batter, then leave to stand for 10 minutes.

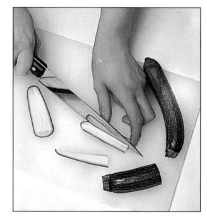

5 To make the Thai salsa, mix all the ingredients together in a bowl.

6 Heat the wok, then add the remaining oil. When the oil is hot, stir-fry the zucchini in batches. Drain well on paper towels, then serve hot with the salsa, garnished with fresh mint sprigs.

Spiced Coconut Mushrooms

Here is a simple and delicious way to cook mushrooms. They may be served with almost any Asian meal as well as with grilled or roasted meats and poultry.

Serves 3-4

INGREDIENTS
2 tbsp peanut oil
2 garlic cloves, finely chopped
2 fresh red chilies, seeded and
   sliced into rings
3 shallots, finely chopped
225 g/8 oz crimini or button
   mushrooms, thickly sliced
⅔ cup coconut milk
2 tbsp fresh cilantro,
   finely chopped
salt and ground black pepper

red chilies

coconut milk

mushrooms

peanut oil

cilantro

garlic

1 Heat a wok until hot, add the oil and swirl it around. Add the garlic and chilies, then stir-fry for a few seconds.

2 Add the shallots and stir-fry for 2–3 minutes, until softened. Add the mushrooms and stir-fry for 3 minutes.

3 Pour in the coconut milk and bring to a boil. Boil rapidly over high heat until the liquid is reduced by half and coats the mushrooms. Taste and adjust the seasoning, if necessary.

4 Sprinkle over the cilantro and toss gently to mix. Serve at once.

VARIATION
Use chopped fresh chives instead of cilantro if you wish.

Marinated Mixed Vegetables with Basil Oil

Basil oil is a must for drizzling over plain stir-fried vegetables. Once it has been made up, it will keep in the fridge for up to 2 weeks.

Serves 2–4 as an accompaniment

INGREDIENTS

1 tbsp olive oil
1 clove garlic, crushed
rind of 1 lemon, finely grated
1 × 14 oz can artichoke hearts, drained and rinsed
2 large leeks, sliced
8 oz patty pan squash, halved if large
4 oz plum tomatoes, cut into segments lengthwise
½ oz basil leaves
⅔ cup extra-virgin olive oil
salt and freshly ground black pepper

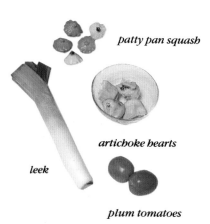

patty pan squash

artichoke hearts

leek

plum tomatoes

1 Mix together the olive oil, garlic and lemon rind in a bowl, to make a marinade.

2 Place the artichokes, leeks, patty pan squash and plum tomatoes in a large bowl, pour over the marinade and leave for 30 minutes.

3 Meanwhile, make the basil oil. Blend the basil leaves with the extra-virgin olive oil in a food processor until puréed.

4 Heat the wok, then stir-fry the marinated vegetables for 3–4 minutes, tossing well. Drizzle the basil oil over the vegetables and serve.

Spicy Potatoes and Cauliflower

This dish is simplicity itself to make and may be eaten as a vegetarian main meal for two with Indian breads or rice, a raita, such as cucumber and yogurt, and a fresh mint relish.

Serves 2

INGREDIENTS
8 oz potatoes
5 tbsp peanut oil
1 tsp ground cumin
1 tsp ground coriander
¼ tsp ground turmeric
¼ tsp cayenne pepper
1 fresh green chili, seeded and
   finely chopped
1 medium cauliflower, broken up
   into small florets
1 tsp cumin seeds
2 garlic cloves, cut into shreds
1-2 tbsp fresh coriander
   finely chopped
salt, to taste

potatoes

cumin seeds   cayenne pepper

cilantro

coriander   turmeric

cauliflower

cumin   garlic
green chili

1   Boil the potatoes in their skins in boiling, salted water for about 20 minutes, until just tender. Drain and let cool. When cool enough to handle, peel and cut into 1-in cubes.

2   Heat 3 tbsp of the oil in a kadhai or wok. When hot, add the ground cumin, coriander, turmeric, cayenne pepper and chili. Let the spices sizzle for a few seconds.

3   Add the cauliflower and about 4 tbsp water. Cook, stirring continuously, for 6–8 minutes over medium heat. Add the potatoes and stir-fry for 2–3 minutes. Season to taste, then remove from the heat.

4   Heat the remaining oil in a small frying pan. When hot, add the cumin seeds and garlic and cook until lightly browned. Pour the mixture over the vegetables. Sprinkle with the chopped cilantro and serve at once.

Stir-fried Chickpeas

Buy canned chickpeas and you will save all the time needed for soaking and then thoroughly cooking dried chickpeas. Served with a crisp green salad, this dish makes a filling vegetarian main course for two, or could be served in smaller quantities as a starter or side dish.

Serves 2–4 as an accompaniment

INGREDIENTS
2 tbsp sunflower seeds
1 × 14 oz can chickpeas, drained
    and rinsed
1 tsp chili powder
1 tsp paprika
2 tbsp vegetable oil
1 clove garlic, crushed
7 oz canned chopped tomatoes
8 oz fresh spinach, well washed and
    coarse stalks removed
salt and freshly ground black pepper
2 tsp chili oil

spinach

garlic

sunflower seeds

chickpeas

1 Heat the wok, and then add the sunflower seeds. Dry-fry until the seeds are golden and toasted.

2 Remove the sunflower seeds and set aside. Toss the chickpeas in chili powder and paprika. Remove and reserve.

3 Heat the wok, then add the oil. When the oil is hot, stir-fry the garlic for 30 seconds, add the chickpeas and stir-fry for 1 minute.

4 Stir in the tomatoes and stir-fry for 4 minutes. Toss in the spinach, season well and stir-fry for 1 minute. Drizzle chili oil and scatter sunflower seeds over the vegetables, then serve.

Red-cooked Tofu with Chinese Mushrooms

Red-cooked is a term applied to Chinese dishes cooked with dark soy sauce. This tasty dish can be served as either a side dish or main meal.

Serves 2-4

INGREDIENTS

8 oz firm tofu
3 tbsp dark soy sauce
2 tbsp Chinese rice wine or
    medium-dry sherry
2 tsp dark brown sugar
1 garlic clove, crushed
1 tbsp fresh ginger,
    finely grated
2.5 ml/½ tsp Chinese five-
    spice powder
pinch of ground roasted
    Szechuan peppercorns
6 dried Chinese black mushrooms
1 tsp cornstarch
2 tbsp peanut oil
5-6 scallions, sliced into
    1-in lengths
rice noodles, to serve
small basil leaves, to garnish

1 Drain the tofu, pat dry with paper towels and cut into 1-in cubes. Place in a shallow dish. In a small bowl, mix together the soy sauce, rice wine or sherry, sugar, garlic, ginger, five-spice powder and Szechuan peppercorns. Pour the marinade over the tofu, toss well and let marinate for about 30 minutes. Drain, reserving the marinade.

2 Meanwhile, soak the dried black mushrooms in warm water for 20–30 minutes until soft. Drain, reserving 6 tbsp of the soaking liquid. Squeeze out any excess liquid from the mushrooms, remove the tough stalks and slice the caps. In a small bowl, blend the cornstarch with the reserved marinade and mushroom soaking liquid.

3 Heat a wok until hot, add the oil and swirl it around. Add the tofu and fry for 2–3 minutes, until evenly golden. Remove from the wok and set aside.

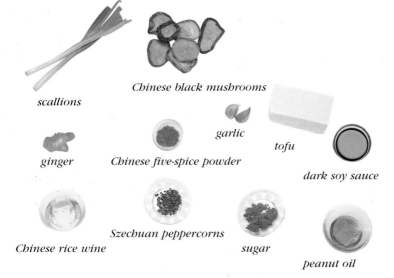

scallions

Chinese black mushrooms

garlic

tofu

ginger

Chinese five-spice powder

dark soy sauce

Chinese rice wine

Szechuan peppercorns

sugar

peanut oil

4 Add the mushrooms and white scallions to the wok and stir-fry for 2 minutes. Pour in the marinade mixture and stir for 1 minute, until thickened.

5 Return the tofu to the wok with the green scallions. Simmer gently for 1–2 minutes. Serve at once with rice noodles and sprinkled with basil leaves.

Mixed Roasted Vegetables

Frying Parmesan cheese in this unusual way gives
a wonderful crusty coating to the vegetables and
creates a truly Mediterranean flavor.

*Serves 4 as an
accompaniment*

INGREDIENTS
1 large eggplant, about 8 oz
salt, for sprinkling
6 oz plum tomatoes
2 red peppers
1 yellow pepper
2 tbsp olive oil
1 oz Parmesan cheese
2 tbsp fresh parsley, chopped
freshly ground black pepper

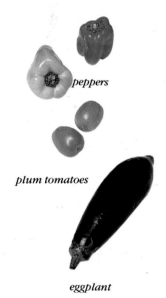

peppers

plum tomatoes

eggplant

1 Cut the eggplant into segments lengthwise. Place in a colander and sprinkle with salt. Leave for 30 minutes, to allow the salt to draw out the bitter juices.

2 Rinse off the salt under cold water and pat dry on paper towels.

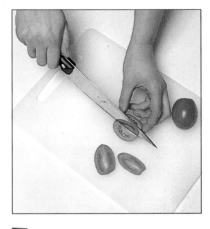

3 Cut the plum tomatoes into segments lengthwise.

4 Cut the red and yellow peppers into quarters lengthwise and deseed.

5 Heat the wok, then add 1 tsp of the olive oil. When the oil is hot, add the Parmesan and stir-fry until golden brown. Remove from the wok, allow to cool and chop into fine flakes.

6 Heat the wok, and then add the remaining oil. When the oil is hot stir-fry the eggplant and peppers for 4–5 minutes. Stir in the tomatoes and stir-fry for a further 1 minute. Toss the vegetables in the Parmesan, parsley and black pepper and serve.

Jicama, Beet and Carrot Stir-fry

This is a dazzling colorful dish with a crunchy texture and fragrant taste.

Serves 4 as an accompaniment

INGREDIENTS
¼ cup pine nuts
4 oz jicama, peeled
4 oz beets, peeled
4 oz carrots, peeled
1½ tbsp vegetable oil
juice of 1 orange
2 tbsp fresh coriander, chopped
salt and freshly ground black pepper

pine nuts

carrot

jicama

beet

1 Heat the wok, then add the pine nuts and toss until golden brown. Remove and set on one side.

2 Cut the jicama, beets and carrots into long thin strips.

3 Heat the wok and add one-third of the oil. When the oil is hot, stir-fry the jicama, beets and carrots for 2–3 minutes. Remove and set aside.

4 Pour the orange juice into the wok and simmer for 2 minutes. Remove and keep warm.

5 Arrange the vegetables in bundles, and sprinkle over the coriander and salt and pepper.

6 Drizzle over the orange juice, sprinkle in the pine nuts, and serve.

Bok Choy and Mushroom Stir-fry

Try to buy all the varieties of mushroom for this dish; the wild oyster and shiitake mushrooms have particularly distinctive, delicate flavors.

Serves 4 as an accompaniment

INGREDIENTS
4 dried black Chinese mushrooms
1 lb bok choy
2 oz oyster mushrooms
2 oz shiitake mushrooms
1 tbsp vegetable oil
1 clove garlic, crushed
2 tbsp oyster sauce

Chinese mushrooms

shiitake mushrooms

bok choy

oyster mushrooms

1 Soak the black Chinese mushrooms in ⅔ cup boiling water for 15 minutes to soften them.

2 Tear the bok choy into bite-size pieces with your fingers.

3 Halve any large oyster or shiitake mushrooms, using a sharp knife.

4 Strain the Chinese mushrooms. Heat the wok, then add the oil. When the oil is hot, stir-fry the garlic until softened but not colored.

5 Add the bok choy and stir-fry for 1 minute. Mix in all the mushrooms and stir-fry for 1 minute.

6 Add the oyster sauce, toss well and serve immediately.

Spicy ChickPeas with Fresh Ginger

Chickpeas are filling, nourishing and cheap. Here they are served with a refreshing raita made with scallions and mint. Serve as a snack or as part of a main meal.

Serves 4-6

INGREDIENTS

8 oz dried chickpeas
2 tbsp vegetable oil
1 small onion, chopped
1½-in piece fresh ginger, finely chopped
2 garlic cloves, finely chopped
¼ tsp ground turmeric
1 lb tomatoes, peeled, seeded and chopped
2 tbsp cilantro, finely chopped
2 tsp garam masala
salt and pepper
fresh cilantro sprigs, to garnish

FOR THE RAITA

⅔ cup plain yogurt
2 scallions, finely chopped
1 tsp roasted cumin seeds
2 tbsp chopped fresh mint
pinch of cayenne pepper, or to taste

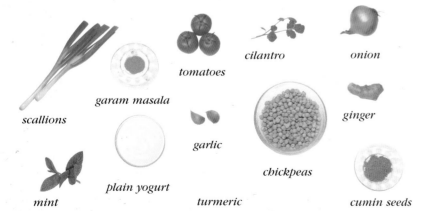

scallions

garam masala

tomatoes

cilantro

onion

mint

plain yogurt

garlic

chickpeas

ginger

turmeric

cumin seeds

VARIATION
You can replace the dried chickpeas with 2 x 15-oz cans chickpeas. Drain and rinse thoroughly before adding to the tomatoes in step 3.

1 Put the chickpeas in a large bowl and pour over enough cold water to cover. Allow to soak overnight. The next day, drain the chickpeas and put them in a large pan with fresh cold water to cover. Bring to a boil, then boil hard for 10 minutes. Lower the heat and simmer gently for 1½–2 hours, until tender. Drain well.

2 Heat a kadhai or wok until hot, add the oil and swirl it around. Add the onion and stir-fry for 2–3 minutes, then add the ginger, garlic and turmeric. Stir-fry for a few seconds more.

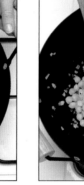

3 Add the tomatoes, chickpeas and seasoning, bring to a boil, then simmer for 10–15, until the tomatoes have reduced to a thick sauce.

4 Meanwhile, make the raita: mix together the yogurt, scallions, roasted cumin seeds, mint and cayenne pepper to taste. Set aside.

5 Just before the end of cooking, stir the chopped cilantro and garam masala into the chickpeas. Serve at once, garnished with cilantro sprigs and accompanied by the raita.

Bean Curd Stir-fry

The bean curd has a pleasant creamy texture, which contrasts well with crunchy stir-fried vegetables. Make sure that you buy firm bean curd, as this is easy to cut neatly.

Serves 2–4

INGREDIENTS
4 oz cabbage
2 green chilies
8 oz firm bean curd
3 tbsp vegetable oil
2 cloves garlic, crushed
3 scallions, chopped
6 oz green beans, topped and tailed
6 oz baby corn, halved
4 oz bean sprouts
3 tbsp smooth peanut butter
1½ tbsp dark soy sauce
1¼ cups coconut milk

baby corn

bean sprouts

chili

bean curd

green beans

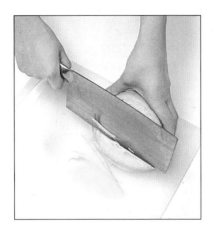

1 Shred the cabbage. Carefully remove the seeds from the chilies and chop finely. Wear rubber gloves to protect your hands, if necessary.

2 Cut the bean curd into strips.

3 Heat the wok, then add 2 tbsp of the oil. When the oil is hot, add the bean curd, stir-fry for 3 minutes and remove. Set aside. Wipe out the wok with paper towels.

4 Add the remaining oil. When it is hot, add the garlic, scallions and chilies and stir-fry for 1 minute. Add the green beans, corn and bean sprouts and stir-fry for a further 2 minutes.

5 Add the peanut butter and soy sauce. Stir well to coat the vegetables. Add the bean curd to the vegetables.

6 Pour the coconut milk over the vegetables, simmer for 3 minutes and serve immediately.

Black Bean and Vegetable Stir-fry

The secret of a quick stir-fry is to prepare all the ingredients first. This colorful vegetable mixture is coated in a classic Chinese sauce.

Serves 4

INGREDIENTS
8 scallions
2 cups button mushrooms
1 red bell pepper
1 green bell pepper
2 large carrots
4 tbsp sesame oil
2 garlic cloves, crushed
4 tbsp black bean sauce
6 tbsp warm water
8 oz beansprouts
salt and freshly ground black pepper

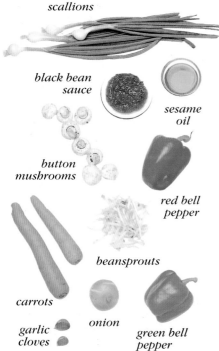

scallions

black bean sauce

sesame oil

button mushrooms

red bell pepper

beansprouts

carrots

garlic cloves

onion

green bell pepper

1 Thinly slice the scallions and button mushrooms. Set them to one side in separate bowls.

2 Cut both the bell peppers in half. Remove the seeds, and slice the flesh into thin strips.

3 Cut the carrots in half. Cut each half into thin strips lengthwise. Stack the slices, and cut through them to make very fine strips.

4 Heat the oil in a large wok or frying pan until very hot. Add the scallions and garlic, and stir-fry for 30 seconds.

5 Add the mushrooms, bell peppers and carrots. Stir-fry for 5–6 minutes over a high heat until the vegetables are just beginning to soften.

6 Mix the black bean sauce with the water. Add to the wok or pan, and cook for 3–4 minutes. Stir in the beansprouts, and stir-fry for 1 minute more, until all the vegetables are coated in the sauce. Season to taste. Serve at once.

COOK'S TIP
For best results the oil in the wok must be very hot before adding the vegetables.

Lentil Stir-fry

Mushrooms, artichokes, sugar snap peas and lentils make a satisfying stir-fry supper.

Serves 2–3

INGREDIENTS

4 oz sugar snap peas
1 oz butter
1 small onion, chopped
4 oz cup or button mushrooms,
  sliced
14 oz can artichoke hearts,
  drained and halved
14 oz can green lentils, drained
4 tbsp light cream
¼ cup shaved almonds, toasted
salt and freshly ground black pepper
French bread, to serve

light cream *green lentils*

cup mushrooms

sugar snap peas

shaved almonds

artichoke hearts

onion

COOK'S TIP
Use strained, plain yogurt instead of the cream, if you like.

1 Bring a pan of salted water to a boil. Add the sugar snap peas, and cook for about 4 minutes until just tender. Drain, and refresh under cold running water. Then drain again. Pat dry the peas with paper towels, and set aside.

2 Melt the butter in a frying pan. Add the chopped onion and cook for 2–3 minutes, stirring occasionally.

3 Add the sliced mushrooms to the onion. Stir until combined. Then cook for 2–3 minutes until just tender. Add the artichokes, sugar snap peas and lentils to the pan. Stir-fry for 2 minutes.

4 Stir in the cream and almonds, and cook for 1 minute. Season to taste. Serve at once, with chunks of French bread.

Vegetable Fajita

A colorful medley of mushrooms and bell peppers in a spicy sauce, wrapped in tortillas and served with creamy guacamole.

Serves 2

INGREDIENTS
1 onion
1 red bell pepper
1 green bell pepper
1 yellow bell pepper
1 garlic clove, crushed
8 oz mushrooms
6 tbsp vegetable oil
2 tbsp medium chili powder
salt and freshly ground black pepper

FOR THE GUACAMOLE
1 ripe avocado
1 shallot, coarsely chopped
1 green chili, seeded and
  coarsely chopped
juice of 1 lime

TO SERVE
4–6 flour tortillas, warmed
1 lime, cut into wedges
cilantro sprigs

green bell pepper   *yellow bell pepper*   *red bell pepper*

mushrooms   *green chili*

garlic clove   *shallot*

avocado

lime   *chili powder*   *onion*

1 Slice the onion. Cut the bell peppers in half, remove the seeds, and cut the flesh into strips. Combine the onion and peppers in a bowl. Add the crushed garlic, and mix lightly.

2 Remove the mushroom stalks. Save for making stock, or discard. Slice the mushroom caps, and add to the pepper mixture in the bowl. Mix the oil and chili powder in a cup, pour over the vegetable mixture, and stir well. Set aside.

3 Make the guacamole. Cut the avocado in half, and remove the pit and the peel. Put the flesh into a food processor or blender with the shallot, green chili and lime juice. Process for 1 minute until smooth. Scrape into a small bowl, cover tightly, and put in the fridge to chill until required.

4 Heat a frying pan or wok until very hot. Add the marinated vegetables, and stir-fry over a high heat for 5–6 minutes until the mushrooms and pepper are just tender. Season well. Spoon a little of the filling on to each tortilla, and roll up. Garnish with fresh cilantro, and serve with the guacamole and lime wedges.

Crispy Noodles with Mixed Vegetables

In this dish, rice vermicelli noodles are deep-fried until crisp, then tossed into a colorful selection of stir-fried vegetables.

COOK'S TIP
If a milder flavor is preferred, remove the seeds from the chili.

Serves 3-4

INGREDIENTS
2 large carrots
2 zucchini
4 scallions
4 oz Chinese long beans or green beans
4 oz dried vermicelli rice noodles or cellophane noodles
peanut oil, for deep frying
1-in piece fresh ginger, cut into shreds
1 fresh red chili, sliced
4 oz fresh shiitake or button mushrooms, thickly sliced
few Chinese cabbage leaves, coarsely shredded
3 oz beansprouts
2 tbsp light soy sauce
2 tbsp Chinese rice wine
1 tsp sugar
2 tbsp cilantro leaves, coarsely torn

scallions

mushrooms

Chinese long beans

cilantro

beansprouts

red chilies

carrot

Chinese cabbage

zucchini

ginger

Chinese rice wine

light soy sauce

1 Cut the carrots and zucchini into fine sticks, and then shred the scallions into similar-size pieces. Trim the beans. If using Chinese long beans, cut them into short lengths.

2 Break the noodles into lengths of about 3 in. Half-fill a wok with oil and heat it to 350°F. Deep-fry the raw noodles, about a handful at a time, for 1–2 minutes, until puffed and crispy. Drain on paper towels. Carefully pour off all but 2 tbsp of the oil.

3 Reheat the oil in the wok. When hot, add the beans and stir-fry for 2–3 minutes. Add the ginger, red chili, mushrooms, carrots and zucchini and stir-fry for 1–2 minutes.

4 Add the Chinese cabbage, beansprouts and scallions Stir-fry for 1 minute, then add the soy sauce, rice wine and sugar. Cook, stirring, for about 30 seconds.

5 Add the noodles and cilantro and toss to mix, taking care not to crush the noodles too much. Serve at once, piled up on a plate.

Nasi Goreng

This dish is originally from Thailand, but can easily be adapted by adding any cooked ingredients you have to hand. Crispy shrimp crackers make an ideal accompaniment.

Serves 4

INGREDIENTS
8 oz long grain rice
2 large eggs
2 tbsp vegetable oil
1 green chili
2 scallions, roughly chopped
2 cloves garlic, crushed
8 oz cooked chicken
8 oz cooked shrimp
3 tbsp dark soy sauce
shrimp crackers, to serve

rice

soy sauce

egg

chili

shrimp

1 Rinse the rice and then cook for 10–12 minutes in 2 cups water in a saucepan with a tight-fitting lid. When cooked, refresh under cold water.

2 Lightly beat the eggs. Heat 1 tbsp of oil in a small frying pan and swirl in the beaten egg. When cooked on one side, flip over and cook on the other side, remove from the pan and leave to cool. Cut the omelet into strips.

3 Carefully remove the seeds from the chili and chop finely, wearing rubber gloves to protect your hands if necessary. Place the scallions, chili and garlic in a food processor and blend to a paste.

4 Heat the wok, and then add the remaining oil. When the oil is hot, add the paste and stir-fry for 1 minute.

5 Add the chicken and shrimp.

6 Add the rice and stir-fry for 3–4 minutes. Stir in the soy sauce and serve with shrimp crackers.

Thai Fried Rice

This hot and spicy dish is easy to prepare and makes a meal in itself.

Serves 4

INGREDIENTS

8 oz Thai jasmine rice
3 tbsp vegetable oil
1 onion, chopped
1 small red bell pepper, seeded
  and cut into ¾-in cubes
12 oz skinless and boneless
  chicken breasts, cut into
  ¾-in cubes
1 garlic clove, crushed
1 tbsp mild curry paste
½ tsp paprika
½ tsp ground turmeric
2 tbsp Thai fish sauce
  (*nam pla*)
2 eggs, beaten
salt and ground black pepper
fried basil leaves, to garnish

rice

Thai fish sauce

chicken

curry paste

onion

egg

red pepper

turmeric

paprika

vegetable oil

VARIATION
Add 2 oz frozen peas to the chicken in step 3, if you wish.

 Put the rice in a sieve and wash thoroughly under cold running water. Then put the rice in a heavy-bottomed pan and add 6¼ cups boiling water. Return to a boil, then simmer, leaving the pan uncovered, for 8–10 minutes; drain well. Spread out the grains on a tray and set aside to cool.

2 Heat a wok until hot, add 2 tbsp of the oil and swirl it around. Add the onion and red pepper and stir-fry for 1 minute.

3 Add the chicken, garlic, curry paste and spices and stir-fry for 2–3 minutes.

4 Reduce the heat to medium, add the cooled rice, fish sauce and seasoning. Stir-fry for 2–3 minutes, until the rice is very hot.

5 Make a well in the center of the rice and add the remaining oil. When hot, add the beaten eggs, allow to cook for about 2 minutes until lightly set, then stir into the rice.

6 Sprinkle over the fried basil leaves and serve at once.

Stir-fried Noodles with Sweet Soy Salmon

Teriyaki sauce forms the marinade for the salmon in this recipe. Served with soft-fried noodles, it makes a stunning dish.

Serves 4

INGREDIENTS
12 oz salmon fillet
2 tbsp Japanese soy
    sauce (*shoyu*)
2 tbsp sake
4 tbsp mirin or
    sweet sherry
1 tsp light brown sugar
2 tsp fresh ginger
    finely grated
3 garlic cloves, 1 crushed, and
    2 sliced into rounds
2 tbsp peanut oil
8 oz dried egg noodles,
    cooked and drained
2 oz alfalfa sprouts
2 tbsp sesame seeds,
    lightly toasted

garlic

sesame seeds

noodles

alfalfa sprouts

sake

mirin

salmon

sugar

Japanese soy sauce

peanut oil

ginger

COOK'S TIP

It is important to scrape the marinade off the fish as any remaining pieces of ginger or garlic would burn during broiling and spoil the finished dish.

1 Thinly slice the salmon, then place in a shallow dish.

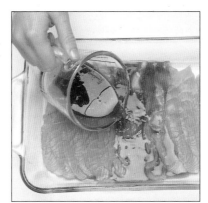

2 In a bowl, mix together the soy sauce, sake, mirin or sherry, sugar, ginger and crushed garlic. Pour over the salmon, cover and leave for 30 minutes.

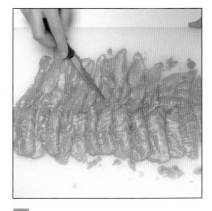

3 Preheat the broiler. Drain the salmon, scraping off and reserving the marinade. Place the salmon in a single layer on a baking sheet. Cook under the broiler for 2–3 minutes without turning.

4 Meanwhile, heat a wok until hot, add the oil and swirl it around. Add the garlic rounds and cook until golden brown but not burnt.

5 Add the cooked noodles and reserved marinade to the wok and stir-fry for 3–4 minutes, until the marinade has reduced slightly to a syrupy glaze and coats the noodles.

6 Toss in the alfalfa sprouts, then remove immediately from the heat. Transfer to warmed serving plates and top with the salmon. Sprinkle over the toasted sesame seeds. Serve at once.

Nutty Rice and Mushroom Stir-fry

This delicious and substantial supper dish can be eaten hot or cold with salads.

Serves 4–6

INGREDIENTS

12 oz long grain rice
3 tbsp sunflower oil
1 small onion, roughly chopped
8 oz field mushrooms, sliced
½ cup hazelnuts, roughly chopped
½ cup pecans, roughly chopped
½ cup almonds, roughly chopped
4 tbsp fresh parsley, chopped
salt and freshly ground black pepper

rice

almonds

field mushroom

hazelnuts

pecans

1 Rinse the rice, then cook for about 10–12 minutes in 2½–3 cups water in a saucepan with a tight-fitting lid. When cooked, refresh under cold water. Heat the wok, then add half the oil. When the oil is hot, stir-fry the rice for 2–3 minutes. Remove and set aside.

2 Add the remaining oil and stir-fry the onion for 2 minutes until softened.

3 Mix in the field mushrooms and stir-fry for 2 minutes.

4 Add all the nuts and stir-fry for 1 minute. Return the rice to the wok and stir-fry for 3 minutes. Season with salt and pepper. Stir in the parsley and serve.

Mee Krob

This delicious dish makes a filling meal. Take care when frying vermicelli as it has a tendency to spit when added to hot oil.

Serves 4

INGREDIENTS

½ cup vegetable oil
8 oz rice vermicelli
5 oz green beans, topped, tailed and
  halved lengthwise
1 onion, finely chopped
2 boneless, skinless chicken breasts,
  about 6 oz each, cut into strips
1 tsp chili powder
8 oz cooked shrimp
3 tbsp dark soy sauce
3 tbsp white wine vinegar
2 tsp superfine sugar
fresh coriander sprigs, to garnish

rice vermicelli

chicken breast

onion

green beans

shrimp

1 Heat the wok, then add 4 tbsp of the oil. Break up the vermicelli into 3 in lengths. When the oil is hot, fry the vermicelli in batches. Remove from the heat and keep warm.

2 Heat the remaining oil in the wok, then add the green beans, onion and chicken and stir-fry for 3 minutes until the chicken is cooked.

3 Sprinkle in the chili powder. Stir in the shrimp, soy sauce, vinegar and sugar, and stir-fry for 2 minutes.

4 Serve the chicken, shrimp and vegetables on the vermicelli, garnished with sprigs of fresh coriander.

Fried Singapore Noodles

Thai fish cakes vary in their size, and their hotness. You can buy them from Oriental supermarkets, but, if you cannot get hold of them, simply omit them from the recipe.

Serves 4

INGREDIENTS
6 oz rice noodles
4 tbsp vegetable oil
½ tsp salt
3 oz cooked shrimp
6 oz cooked pork, cut into
   matchsticks
1 green pepper, seeded and chopped
   into matchsticks
½ tsp sugar
2 tsp curry powder
3 oz Thai fish cakes
2 tsp dark soy sauce

rice noodles

pork

pepper

shrimp

1 Soak the rice noodles in water for about 10 minutes, drain well, then pat dry with paper towels.

2 Heat the wok, then add half the oil. When the oil is hot, add the noodles and salt and stir-fry for 2 minutes. Transfer to a heated serving dish to keep warm.

3 Heat the remaining oil and add the shrimp, pork, pepper, sugar, curry powder and remaining salt. Stir-fry the ingredients for 1 minute.

4 Return the noodles to the pan and stir-fry with the Thai fish cakes for 2 minutes. Stir in the soy sauce and serve.

Oriental Vegetable Noodles

Thin Italian egg pasta is a good alternative to Oriental egg noodles; use it fresh or dried.

Serves 6

INGREDIENTS
1¼ lb thin tagliarini
1 red onion
4 oz shiitake mushrooms
3 tbsp sesame oil
3 tbsp dark soy sauce
1 tbsp balsamic vinegar
2 tsp superfine sugar
1 tsp salt
celery leaves, to garnish

tagliarini

shiitake mushrooms

red onion

balsamic vinegar

soy sauce

1 Boil the tagliarini in a large pan of salted boiling water, following the instructions on the pack.

2 Thinly slice the red onion and the mushrooms, using a sharp knife.

3 Heat the wok, then add 1 tbsp of the sesame oil. When the oil is hot, stir-fry the onion and mushrooms for 2 minutes.

4 Drain the tagliarini, then add to the wok with the soy sauce, balsamic vinegar, sugar and salt. Stir-fry for 1 minute, then add the remaining sesame oil, and serve garnished with celery leaves.

Chinese Jewelled Rice

This rice dish, with its many different, interesting ingredients, can make a meal in itself.

Serves 4

INGREDIENTS

12 oz long grain rice
3 tbsp vegetable oil
1 onion, roughly chopped
4 oz cooked ham, diced
6 oz canned white crabmeat
3 oz canned water chestnuts, drained
  and cut into cubes
4 dried black Chinese mushrooms,
  soaked, drained and cut into dice
4 oz peas, thawed if frozen
2 tbsp oyster sauce
1 tsp sugar

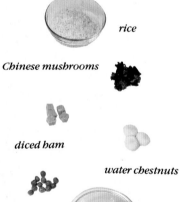
rice

Chinese mushrooms

diced ham

water chestnuts

peas

crabmeat

1 Rinse the rice, then cook for about 10–12 minutes in 2½–3 cups water in a saucepan with a tight-fitting lid. When cooked, refresh under cold water. Heat the wok, then add half the oil. When the oil is hot, stir-fry the rice for 3 minutes, then remove and set aside.

2 Add the remaining oil to the wok. When the oil is hot, cook the onion until softened but not colored.

3 Add all the remaining ingredients and stir-fry for 2 minutes.

4 Return the rice to the wok and stir-fry for 3 minutes, then serve.

Mixed Rice Noodles

A delicious noodle dish made extra special by adding avocado and garnishing with shrimp.

Serves 4

INGREDIENTS

1 tbsp sunflower oil
1 in piece ginger root, peeled
   and grated
2 cloves garlic, crushed
3 tbsp dark soy sauce
8 oz peas, thawed if frozen
1 lb rice noodles
1 lb fresh spinach, well washed and
   coarse stalks removed
2 tbsp smooth peanut butter
2 tbsp tahini
⅔ cup milk
1 ripe avocado, peeled and pitted
roasted peanuts and peeled shrimp,
   to garnish

rice noodles

ginger

peas

peanut butter

spinach

1 Heat the wok, then add the oil. When the oil is fairly hot, stir-fry the ginger and garlic for approximately 30 seconds. Add 1 tbsp of the dark soy sauce and ⅔ cup boiling water.

2 Add the peas and noodles, then cook for 3 minutes. Stir in the spinach. Remove the vegetables and noodles, drain and keep warm.

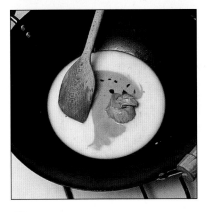

3 Stir the peanut butter, remaining soy sauce, tahini and milk together in the wok, and simmer for 1 minute.

4 Add the vegetables and noodles, slice in the avocado and toss together. Serve piled on individual plates. Spoon some sauce over each portion and garnish with peanuts and shrimp.

Spicy Fried Rice Sticks with Shrimp

This recipe is based on the classic Thai noodle dish called *Pad Thai*. Popular all over Thailand, it is enjoyed morning, noon and night.

Serves 4

INGREDIENTS
½ oz dried shrimp
1 tbsp tamarind pulp
3 tbsp Thai fish sauce
  (*nam pla*)
1 tbsp sugar
2 garlic cloves, chopped
2 fresh red chilies, seeded and
  chopped
3 tbsp peanut oil
2 eggs, beaten
8 oz dried rice sticks, soaked in
  warm water for 30 minutes,
  refreshed under cold running
  water and drained
8 oz cooked peeled
  jumbo shrimp
3 scallions, cut into
  1-in lengths
3 oz beansprouts
2 tbsp coarsely chopped
  roasted unsalted peanuts
2 tbsp fresh cilantro,
  finely chopped
lime slices, to garnish

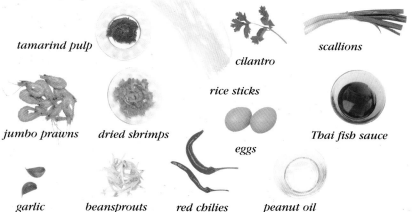

tamarind pulp *cilantro* *scallions* *rice sticks* *jumbo prawns* *dried shrimps* *eggs* *Thai fish sauce* *garlic* *beansprouts* *red chilies* *peanut oil*

VARIATION
For a vegetarian dish omit the dried shrimp and replace the jumbo shrimp with cubes of deep-fried tofu.

1 Put the dried shrimp in a small bowl and pour over enough warm water to cover. Let soak for 30 minutes until soft, then drain.

2 Put the tamarind pulp in a bowl and add 4 tbsp hot water. Blend together, then press through a sieve to extract 2 tbsp thick tamarind water. Mix the tamarind water with the fish sauce and sugar.

3 Using a mortar and pestle, pound the garlic and chilies to form a paste. Heat a wok over medium heat, add 1 tbsp of the oil, then add the beaten eggs and stir for 1–2 minutes, until the eggs are scrambled. Remove and set aside. Wipe the wok clean.

4 Reheat the wok until hot, add the remaining oil, then the chili paste and dried shrimp and stir-fry for 1 minute. Add the rice sticks and tamarind mixture and stir-fry for 3–4 minutes.

5 Add the scrambled eggs, shrimp, scallions, beansprouts, peanuts and cilantro, then stir-fry for 2 minutes, until well mixed. Serve at once, garnishing each portion with lime slices.

Fried Rice with Spices

This dish is mildly spiced, suitable as an accompaniment to any curried dish. The whole spices are not meant to be eaten.

Serves 3–4

INGREDIENTS

1¼ cups basmati rice
½ tsp salt
1 tbsp ghee or butter
8 whole cloves
4 green cardamom pods, bruised
1 bay leaf
3 in cinnamon stick
1 tsp black peppercorns
1 tsp cumin seeds
1 tsp coriander seeds

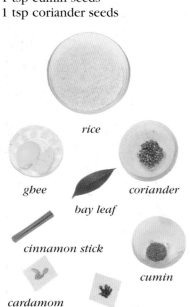

rice

ghee   coriander

bay leaf

cinnamon stick

cumin

cardamom

cloves

VARIATION
You could add ½ tsp ground turmeric to the rice in step 2 to color it yellow.

1 Put the rice in a colander and wash thoroughly under cold running water until the water clears. Put in a bowl and pour 2½ cups fresh water over the rice. Allow the rice to soak for 30 minutes; then drain thoroughly.

2 Put the rice, salt and 2½ cups water in a heavy-bottomed pan. Bring to a boil, then simmer, covered, for about 10 minutes. The rice should be just cooked with still a little bite to it. Drain off any excess water, fluff up the grains with a fork, then spread it out on a tray and let cool.

3 Heat the ghee or butter in a kadhai or wok until foaming, add the spices and stir-fry for 1 minute.

4 Add the cooled rice and stir-fry for 3–4 minutes, until warmed through. Serve at once.

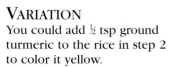

Singapore Noodles

A delicious supper dish with a stunning mix of flavors and textures.

Serves 4

INGREDIENTS

8 oz dried egg noodles
3 tbsp peanut oil
1 onion, chopped
1-in piece fresh ginger,
    finely chopped
1 garlic clove,
    finely chopped
1 tbsp Madras curry powder
½ tsp salt
4 oz cooked chicken or pork,
    finely shredded
4 oz cooked peeled shrimp
4 oz Chinese cabbage leaves,
    shredded
4 oz beansprouts
4 tbsp chicken stock
1-2 tbsp dark soy sauce
1-2 fresh red chilies, seeded
    and finely shredded
4 scallions, finely shredded

beansprouts

Chinese cabbage

noodles

ginger

curry powder

chicken

dark soy sauce

onion

stock

scallions

red chilies

peanut oil

shrimp

1 Cook the noodles according to the package instructions. Rinse thoroughly under cold water and drain well. Toss in 1 tbsp of the oil and set aside.

2 Heat a wok until hot, add the remaining oil and swirl it around. Add the onion, ginger and garlic and stir-fry for about 2 minutes.

3 Add the curry powder and salt, stir-fry for 30 seconds, then add the egg noodles, chicken or pork and shrimp. Stir-fry for 3–4 minutes.

4 Add the Chinese cabbage and beansprouts and stir-fry for 1–2 minutes. Sprinkle in the stock and soy sauce to taste and toss well until evenly mixed. Serve at once, garnished with the shredded red chilies and scallions.

Indonesian Fried Rice

This fried rice dish makes an ideal supper on its own or as an accompaniment.

Serves 4-6

INGREDIENTS
4 shallots, coarsely chopped
1 fresh red chili, seeded
    and chopped
1 garlic clove, chopped
thin sliver of dried shrimp paste
3 tbsp vegetable oil
8 oz boneless lean pork, cut into
    fine strips
1¼ cups long-grain white rice,
    boiled and cooled
3-4 scallions, thinly sliced
4 oz cooked peeled shrimp
2 tbsp sweet soy sauce
    (*kecap manis*)
chopped fresh cilantro and
    fine cucumber shreds,
    to garnish

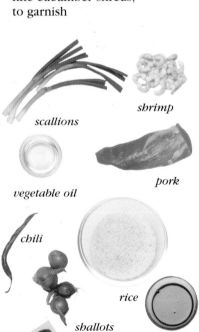

scallions

shrimp

vegetable oil

pork

chili

rice

shallots

soy sauce

dried shrimp paste

garlic

1 In a mortar pound the shallots, chili, garlic and shrimp paste with a pestle until they form a paste.

2 Heat a wok until hot, then add 2 tbsp of the oil and swirl it around. Add the pork and stir-fry for 2–3 minutes. Remove the pork from the wok, set aside and keep warm.

3 Add the remaining oil to the wok. When hot, add the spiced shallot paste and stir-fry for about 30 seconds.

4 Reduce the heat. Add the rice, scallions and shrimp. Stir-fry for 2–3 minutes. Add the pork and sprinkle over the soy sauce. Stir-fry for 1 minute. Serve garnished with the chopped cilantro and cucumber shreds.

Noodles with Ginger and Cilantro

Here is a simple noodle dish that goes well with most Asian dishes. It can also be served as a snack for 2-3 people.

Serves 4-6

INGREDIENTS
handful of fresh cilantro sprigs
8 oz dried egg noodles
3 tbsp peanut oil
2-in piece fresh root ginger, cut
  into fine shreds
6-8 scallions, cut into shreds
2 tbsp light soy sauce
salt and ground black pepper

scallions

peanut oil

ginger

cilantro *noodles*

light soy sauce

COOK'S TIP
Italian noodles are often the easiest to buy. They range in size from very thin to broad. Allow 2 oz per person as a side dish, and up to 4 oz for a main dish.

1 Strip the leaves from the cilantro stalks. Pile them on a chopping board and coarsely chop them, using a cleaver or large sharp knife.

2 Cook the noodles according to the instructions on the package. Rinse under cold water and drain well. Toss in 1 tbsp of the oil.

3 Heat a wok until hot, add the remaining oil and swirl it around. Add the ginger and stir-fry for a few seconds, then add the noodles and scallions. Stir-fry for 3–4 minutes, until hot.

4 Sprinkle over the soy sauce, cilantro and seasoning. Toss well, then serve at once.

Stir-fried Tofu and Beansprouts with Noodles

This is a satisfying dish, which is both tasty and easy to make.

Serves 4

INGREDIENTS

8 oz firm tofu
peanut oil, for deep frying
6 oz medium egg noodles
1 tbsp sesame oil
1 tsp cornstarch
2 tsp dark soy sauce
1 tbsp Chinese rice wine
1 tsp sugar
6–8 scallions, cut diagonally into
  1-in lengths
3 garlic cloves, sliced
1 fresh green chili, seeded
  and sliced
4 oz Chinese cabbage leaves,
  coarsely shredded
2 oz beansprouts
2 oz cashew nuts, toasted

scallions

garlic

sesame oil

Chinese cabbage

tofu

noodles

beansprouts

dark soy sauce

Chinese rice wine

green chili

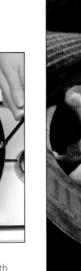

1 Drain the tofu and pat dry with paper towels. Cut the tofu into 1-in cubes. Half-fill a wok with peanut oil and heat to 350°F. Deep-fry the tofu in batches for 1–2 minutes, until golden and crisp. Drain on paper towels. Carefully pour all but 2 tbsp of the oil from the wok.

2 Cook the noodles. Rinse them thoroughly under cold water and drain well. Toss in 2 tsp of the sesame oil and set aside. In a bowl, blend together the cornstarch, soy sauce, rice wine, sugar and remaining sesame oil.

3 Reheat the 2 tbsp of peanut oil and, when hot enough, add the lengths of scallion, sliced garlic, sliced chili, shredded Chinese cabbage and beansprouts. Stir-fry for 1–2 minutes.

4 Add the tofu with the noodles and sauce. Cook, stirring, for about 1 minute, until well mixed. Sprinkle over the cashew nuts. Serve at once.

Chow Mein

One of the most well-known Chinese dishes, this recipe is both easy to prepare and healthy.

Serves 4

INGREDIENTS
8 oz dried egg noodles
2 tbsp oil
1 onion, chopped
½ in fresh ginger root, chopped
2 garlic cloves, crushed
2 tbsp soy sauce
¼ cup dry white wine
2 tsp Chinese five-spice powder
1 lb/4 cups ground pork
4 scallions, sliced
2 oz oyster mushrooms
3 oz bamboo shoots
1 tbsp sesame oil
shrimp crackers, to serve

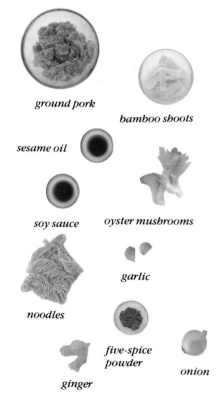

ground pork

bamboo shoots

sesame oil

soy sauce   *oyster mushrooms*

noodles

garlic

five-spice powder   *onion*   *scallions*

ginger

1 Cook the noodles in boiling water for 4 minutes and drain.

2 Meanwhile, heat the oil in a wok and add the onion, ginger, garlic, soy sauce and wine. Cook for 1 minute. Stir in the Chinese five-spice powder.

3 Add the pork and cook for 10 minutes, stirring continuously. Add the scallions, mushrooms, bamboo shoots and continue to cook for a further 5 minutes.

4 Stir in the noodles and sesame oil. Mix all the ingredients together well and serve with shrimp crackers.

Red Fried Rice

This vibrant rice dish owes its appeal as much to the bright colors of red onion, red bell pepper and tomatoes as it does to their flavors.

Serves 2

INGREDIENTS
³/₄ cup basmati rice
2 tbsp peanut oil
1 small red onion, chopped
1 red bell pepper, seeded and
  chopped
8 oz cherry tomatoes, halved
2 eggs, beaten
salt and freshly ground black pepper

eggs

basmati rice

cherry tomatoes

red onion

red bell pepper

1 Wash the rice several times under cold running water. Drain well. Bring a large pan of water to a boil. Add the rice, and cook for 10–12 minutes.

2 Meanwhile, heat the oil in a wok until very hot. Add the onion and red pepper, and stir-fry for 2–3 minutes. Add the cherry tomatoes, and stir-fry for 2 minutes more.

3 Pour in the beaten eggs all at once. Cook for 30 seconds without stirring, then stir to break up the egg as it sets.

4 Drain the cooked rice thoroughly. Add to the wok, and toss it over the heat with the vegetable and egg mixture for 3 minutes. Season the fried rice with salt and pepper to taste.

Fried Noodles with Beansprouts and Asparagus

Soft fried noodles contrast beautifully with crisp beansprouts and asparagus.

Serves 2

INGREDIENTS

4 oz dried egg noodles
4 tbsp vegetable oil
1 small onion, chopped
1 in piece of fresh ginger,
  peeled and grated
2 garlic cloves, crushed
6 oz young asparagus spears,
  trimmed
4 oz beansprouts
4 scallions, sliced
3 tbsp soy sauce
salt and freshly ground black pepper

onion

scallions

garlic cloves

fresh ginger

soy sauce

egg noodles

beansprouts

asparagus spears

1 Bring a pan of salted water to a boil. Add the noodles, and cook for 2–3 minutes, until just tender. Drain, and toss in 2 tbsp of the oil.

2 Heat the remaining oil in a wok or frying pan until very hot. Add the onion, ginger and garlic, and stir-fry for 2–3 minutes. Add the asparagus, and stir-fry for 2–3 minutes more.

3 Add the noodles and beansprouts, and stir-fry for 2 minutes.

4 Stir in the scallions and soy sauce. Season to taste, adding salt sparingly as the soy sauce will probably supply enough salt in itself. Stir-fry for 1 minute, then serve at once.

Five-spice Vegetable Noodles

Vary this vegetable stir-fry by substituting mushrooms, bamboo shoots, beansprouts, snow peas or water chestnuts for some or all of the vegetables suggested below.

Serves 2–3

INGREDIENTS
8 oz dried egg noodles
2 tbsp sesame oil
2 carrots
1 celery stalk
1 small fennel bulb
2 zucchini, halved and sliced
1 red chili, seeded and chopped
1 in piece of fresh ginger, grated
1 garlic clove, crushed
1½ tsp Chinese five-spice powder
½ tsp ground cinnamon
4 scallions, sliced
¼ cup warm water
1 red chili, seed ed and sliced,
   to garnish (optional)

carrots
celery stalk
garlic clove
fennel bulb
egg noodles
zucchini
five-spice powder
scallions
cinnamon
fresh ginger

1 Bring a large pan of salted water to a boil. Add the noodles, and cook for 2–3 minutes until just tender. Drain the noodles, return them to the pan, and toss in a little of the oil. Set aside.

2 Cut the carrot and celery into julienne. Cut the fennel bulb in half, and cut out the hard core. Cut into slices. Then cut the slices into julienne.

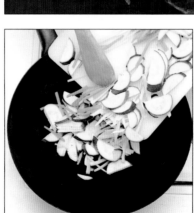

3 Heat the remaining oil in a wok or frying pan until very hot. Add all the vegetables, including the chili, and stir-fry for 7–8 minutes.

4 Add the ginger and garlic, and stir-fry for 2 minutes. Then add the spices. Cook for 1 minute. Add the scallions. Stir-fry for 1 minute. Pour in the warm water, and cook for 1 minute. Stir in the noodles, and toss well together. Serve sprinkled with sliced red chili, if desired.

Stir-fried Vegetables with Pasta

This is a colorful Chinese-style dish, easily prepared using pasta instead of Chinese noodles.

Serves 4

INGREDIENTS
1 medium carrot
6 oz small zucchini
6 oz green beans
6 oz baby corn
1 lb ribbon pasta such as tagliatelle
salt
2 tbsp corn oil, plus extra for tossing
    the pasta
½ in piece fresh ginger, peeled and
    finely chopped
2 garlic cloves, finely chopped
6 tbsp yellow bean sauce
6 scallions, sliced into 1 in lengths
2 tbsp dry sherry
1 tsp sesame seeds

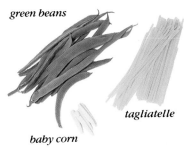

green beans

tagliatelle

baby corn

ginger

scallions

zucchini

garlic

1 Slice the carrot and zucchini diagonally into chunks. Slice the beans diagonally. Cut the baby corn diagonally in half.

2 Cook the pasta in plenty of boiling salted water according to the manufacturer's instructions, drain, then rinse under hot water. Toss in a little oil.

3 Heat 2 tbsp oil until smoking in a wok or skillet and add the ginger and garlic. Stir-fry for 30 seconds, then add the carrots, beans, and zucchini.

4 Stir-fry for 3–4 minutes, then stir in the yellow bean sauce. Stir-fry for 2 minutes, add the scallions, sherry, and pasta and stir-fry for 1 minute more until piping hot. Sprinkle with sesame seeds and serve immediately.

Mango and Coconut Stir-fry

Choose a ripe mango for this recipe. If you buy one that is a little under-ripe, leave it in a warm place for a day or two before using.

Serves 4

INGREDIENTS
¼ coconut
1 large, ripe mango
juice of 2 limes
rind of 2 limes, finely grated
1 tbsp sunflower oil
1 tbsp butter
1½ tbsp honey
sour cream or yogurt, to serve

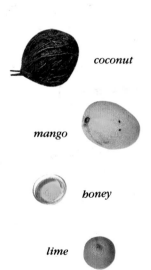

coconut

mango

honey

lime

1 Prepare the coconut shreds by draining the milk from the coconut and shredding the flesh with a peeler.

2 Peel the mango. Cut the pit out of the middle of the fruit. Cut each half of the mango into slices.

COOK'S TIP

Because of the delicate taste of desserts, always make sure your wok has been scrupulously cleaned so there is no transference of flavors – a garlicky mango isn't quite the effect you want to achieve!

3 Place the mango slices in a bowl and pour over the lime juice and rind, to marinate them.

4 Meanwhile, heat the wok, then add 2 tsp of the oil. When the oil is hot, add the butter. When the butter has melted, stir in the coconut shreds and stir-fry for 1–2 minutes until the coconut is golden brown. Remove and drain on paper towels. Wipe out the wok. Strain the mango slices, reserving the juice.

5 Heat the wok and add the remaining oil. When the oil is hot, add the mango and stir-fry for 1–2 minutes, then add the juice and allow to bubble and reduce for 1 minute. Then stir in the honey, sprinkle on the coconut and serve with sour cream or yogurt.

Caramelized Apples

A sweet, sticky dessert which is very quickly made, and usually very quickly eaten!

Serves 4

INGREDIENTS
1½ lb sweet apples
½ cup unsalted butter
1 oz fresh white bread crumbs
½ cup ground almonds
rind of 2 lemons, finely grated
4 tbsp corn syrup
4 tbsp thick strained yogurt,
    to serve

lemon

corn syrup

ground almonds

apple

1 Peel and core the apples.

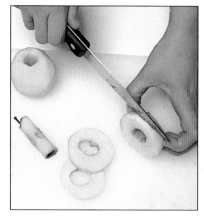

2 Carefully cut the apples into ½ in-thick rings.

3 Heat the wok, then add the butter. When the butter has melted, add the apple rings and stir-fry for 4 minutes until golden and tender. Remove from the wok, reserving the butter. Add the bread crumbs to the hot butter and stir-fry for 1 minute.

4 Stir in the ground almonds and lemon rind and stir-fry for a further 3 minutes, stirring constantly. Sprinkle the breadcrumb mix over the apples, then drizzle warmed corn syrup over the top. Serve with thick strained yogurt.

Crispy Cinnamon Toasts

This recipe is based on a sweet version of French toast. You can use fancy cutters to create a pretty dessert or, if you do not have cutters, simply cut the crusts off the bread and cut it into little fingers.

Serves 4

INGREDIENTS
2 oz raisins
3 tbsp Grand Marnier
4 medium slices white bread
3 medium eggs, beaten
1 tbsp ground cinnamon
2 large oranges
1½ tbsp sunflower oil
2 tbsp unsalted butter
1 tbsp raw sugar
thick strained yogurt, to serve

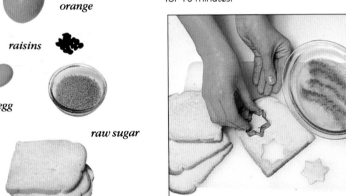

orange

raisins

egg

raw sugar

bread

1 Soak the raisins in the Grand Marnier for 10 minutes.

2 Cut the bread into shapes with a cutter. Place the shapes in a bowl with the eggs and cinnamon to soak.

3 Peel the oranges. Remove any excess pith from the peel, then cut it into fine strips and blanch. Refresh it in cold water, then drain.

4 Strain the raisins. Heat the wok, then add the oil. When the oil is hot, stir in the butter until melted, then add the bread and fry, turning once, until golden brown. Stir in the raisins and orange rind, and sprinkle with sugar. Serve warm with thick strained yogurt.

Kentucky Fried Peaches

Never mind your diet, when peaches are this good, it's time for a break!

Serves 4

INGREDIENTS
5 large ripe peaches
4 tbsp butter
2 tbsp brown sugar
3 tbsp Kentucky bourbon
2 pints/5 cups vanilla ice
    cream
½ cup pecan nuts, toasted

PREPARATION TIME
5 minutes

COOKING TIME
10 minutes

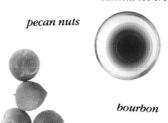

vanilla ice cream

pecan nuts

bourbon

peaches

butter

brown sugar

COOK'S TIP
Peaches that ripen after they are picked will not release their skins when blanched in boiling water.

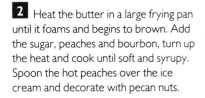

1 Place the peaches in a large bowl and cover with boiling water to loosen their skins. Drain, refresh under cold running water and slice.

2 Heat the butter in a large frying pan until it foams and begins to brown. Add the sugar, peaches and bourbon, turn up the heat and cook until soft and syrupy. Spoon the hot peaches over the ice cream and decorate with pecan nuts.

INDEX

A

Apples: caramelized
    apples, 186
Artichokes: veal escalopes
    with artichokes, 85

B

Basil oil: marinated mixed
    vegetables with basil
    oil, 75
Beancurd stir-fry, 152
Beansprouts, 10
    preparing, 18
    stir-fried tofu and
        beansprouts with
        noodles, 178
Beef: beef rendang, 82
    chili beef with
        basil, 88
    oriental beef, 109
    sizzling beef with
        celeriac straw, 116
    spicy beef, 121
    stir-fried beef and
        broccoli, 123
    sukiyaki-style beef, 100
Beet: jicama, beet and carrot
    stir-fry, 146
Black beans: black
    bean and vegetable
    stir-fry, 154–155
    stir-fried squid with black
        bean sauce, 60
Blueberries: stir-fried duck
    with blueberries, 97
Bok choy: Chinese greens
    with oyster sauce, 132
    fish balls with Chinese
        greens, 54
Bread: crispy cinnamon
    toasts, 188
Broccoli: stir-fried beef
    and broccoli, 123

Buffalo-style chicken
    wings, 114

C

Cabbage: crispy
    cabbage, 128
Carrots: jicama, beet and
    carrot stir-fry, 146
Cashew nuts: glazed
    chicken with cashew
    nuts, 90
Cauliflower: spicy
    potatoes and
    cauliflower, 140
Celeriac: sizzling beef
    with celeriac
    straw, 116
Chicken: Buffalo-style
    chicken wings, 114
    chicken teriyaki, 103
    chicken tikka
        masala, 94
    corn and chicken soup, 41
    glazed chicken with
        cashew nuts, 90
    Indonesian-style satay
        chicken, 86
    mee krob, 167
    mini spring rolls, 26

nasi goreng, 166
    sesame seed chicken
        bites, 31
    spiced honey chicken
        wings, 96
    stir-fried sweet and sour
        chicken, 122
    stock, 22
    Thai red chicken
        curry, 106
    warm stir-fried salad, 54
Chicken liver stir-fry, 80
Chickpeas: spicy chickpeas
    with ginger, 150
    stir-fried chickpeas, 141
Chilies, 12
    flowers, 21
    removing seeds from, 26
Chinese chives: sea bass
    with Chinese chives, 65
Chinese greens with oyster
    sauce, 132
Chinese jewelled rice, 170
Cilantro, 12
    stir-fried vegetables with
        cilantro omelet, 126
Cinnamon: crispy cinnamon
    toasts, 188
Coconut: creamed, 14

fresh coconut milk, 22
    mango and coconut
        stir-fry, 184
    spiced coconut
        mushrooms, 138
    spiced shrimp with
        coconut, 64
    spiced vegetables with
        coconut, 130
    spicy crab and
        coconut, 69
Coriander: coriander
    seeds, 12

noodles with ginger and
    coriander, 177
Corn, 10
    corn and chicken soup, 41
Crab: hot spicy crab
    claws, 50
    Chinese jewelled
        rice, 170
    spicy crab and
        coconut, 69
Crispy cinnamon
    toasts, 188
Crispy "seaweed" with
    flaked almonds, 30
Crispy spring rolls with
    sweet chili dipping
    sauce, 44
Cucumber, 10
    fan, 21
Cumin, 12
Curry: chicken tikka
    masala, 94
    green seafood
        curry, 62
    Thai green curry
        paste, 22
    Thai red chicken
        curry, 106
    Thai red curry paste, 22

D

Duck: duck and ginger chop
    suey, 93
    stir-fried duck with
        blueberries, 97
    sweet-sour duck
        with mango, 110

E

Eggplant: Szechuan
    eggplant, 129

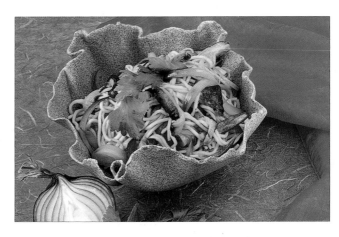

Eggs: stir-fried vegetables
with cilantro omelet, 126
Equipment, 6

F
Fennel, 10
Fish: fish balls with
Chinese greens, 54
fragrant swordfish with
ginger and
lemongrass, 66
green seafood
curry, 62
spicy battered fish, 57
sweet-and-sour fish, 70
Thai fish cakes, 33
Thai fish stir-fry, 72
Thai seafood salad, 51
Fresh produce, 10

G
Galingale, 12
Garam masala, 23
Garlic, 10
lettuce-wrapped garlic
lamb, 28
peeling and
chopping, 18
stir-fried spinach with
garlic and sesame
seeds, 125
Ginger: duck and
ginger chop suey, 93
fragrant swordfish with
ginger and
lemongrass, 66
noodles with ginger and
coriander, 177
oriental scallops with
ginger relish, 78

peeling and
chopping, 20
preparing, 18
root, 12
spicy chickpeas with
ginger, 150
Green seafood
curry, 62

H
Ham: Chinese jewelled
rice, 170
Herbs, 12
Hoisin sauce, 14

I
Indonesian fried
rice, 176
Indonesian-style satay
chicken, 96

J
Jicami, 10
jicami, beet and
carrot stir-fry, 146
preparing, 18

K
Kaffir lime leaves:
preparing, 19

L
Lamb: glazed lamb, 120
lettuce-wrapped garlic
lamb, 28
minted lamb, 102
paper-thin lamb with
scallions, 84
spiced lamb with
spinach, 92

Leeks, 10
Lemongrass, 12
fragrant swordfish with
ginger and
lemongrass, 66
Lemons, 10
pan-fried red snapper
with lemon, 74
Lentil stir-fry, 156
Lettuce-wrapped garlic
lamb, 28
Lime leaves, 12
Limes, 10
Lychees, 10
stir-fried pork with
lychees, 100

M
Mango, 10
mango and coconut
stir-fry, 184
Meat, preparing, 18
Mee krob, 167
Mini spring rolls, 26
Minted lamb, 102
Mushrooms:
bok choi and mushroom
stir-fry, 148
Chinese jewelled rice, 170
nutty rice and mushroom
stir-fry, 166
red-cooked tofu
with Chinese
mushrooms, 142

shiitake, 10
spiced coconut
mushrooms, 138
Mussels: lemongrass-
and-basil-scented
mussels, 56

N
Nasi goreng, 160
Noodles: cellophane
noodles with pork, 115
chow mein, 179
crispy noodles with mixed
vegetables, 158
five spice vegetable
noodles, 182
fried noodles with
beansprouts and
asparagus, 181
fried Singapore
noodles, 168
mixed rice
noodles, 171
noodles with ginger
and coriander, 177
oriental vegetable
noodles, 169
Singapore noodles, 175
spicy fried noodles
with shrimp, 172
stir-fried noodles with
sweet soy salmon, 164
stir-fried tofu and
beansprouts with
noodles, 178

Nuts: mixed spiced nuts, 32
nutty rice and mushrooms
stir-fry, 166

O
Oils, 14
Oriental beef, 109
Oriental scallops with
ginger relish, 78
Oriental vegetable noodles, 169
Oyster sauce, 14

P
Paprika, 12
Parmesan cheese: mixed
roasted vegetables, 144
Parsley, 12
Parsnips: stir-fried
parsnips, 124
Patty pan squash, 10
Peaches: stir-fried
peaches, 189
Peanut butter, 14
Peppers, 10
Pork: cellophane noodles
with pork, 115
Chinese spiced salt
spareribs, 34
fried Singapore
noodles, 168
lemongrass pork, 89
pan-fried pork with
mustard, 112
steamed spiced pork
and water chestnut
wontons, 38
stir-fried pork with
lychees, 108
Potatoes: spicy potatoes and
cauliflower, 140
stir-fried potatoes and
eggs, 40

Q

Quick-fried shrimp
with hot spices, 46

R

Radishes, 10
Red chili sauce, 14
Red snapper: pan-fried red
snapper with lemon, 74
red snapper with ginger
and scallions, 58
Rice: Chinese jewelled
rice, 170
fried rice with spices, 174
Indonesian fried rice, 176
mee krob, 167
mixed rice noodles, 171
nasi goreng, 160
nutty rice and mushroom
stir-fry, 166
red fried rice, 180
Thai fried rice, 162
Rosemary, 12
stir-fried potatoes and
eggs, 40

S

Sage: turkey with sage,
prunes and brandy, 118
Sake, 14
Salad: Thai seafood salad, 51
warm stir-fried salad, 54
Salmon: salmon teriyaki, 52
spiced salmon stir-fry, 76
stir-fried noodles with
sweet soy salmon, 164
Sauces, 14
Scallions: paper-thin
lamb with scallions, 84
red snapper with
ginger and scallions, 58
scallion brush, 21

Scallops: oriental scallops
with ginger
relish, 78
spiced scallops in
their shells, 73
Sea bass with Chinese
chives, 65
Sesame seed chicken
bites, 31
Sherry vinegar, 14
Shrimp: butterfly shrimp, 36
fried Singapore
noodles, 168
green seafood curry, 62
mee krob, 167
nasi goreng, 160
shrimp toasts, 48
quick-fried shrimp with
hot spices, 46
spiced shrimp with
coconut, 64
spicy fried rice sticks
with shrimp, 172
Thai seafood
salad, 51
Soup: corn and chicken
soup, 41
Soy sauce, 14
Spices, 12
Spinach: spiced lamb with
spinach, 92
stir-fried spinach with
garlic and sesame
seeds, 125

Spring greens: crispy
"seaweed" with flaked
almonds, 30
Spring rolls: crispy spring
rolls with sweet chili
dipping sauce, 44
Squid: green seafood
curry, 62
squid with peppers in a
black bean sauce, 68
stir-fried squid with black
bean sauce, 60
Thai seafood
salad, 51
Star anise, 12
Stir-fried potatoes and
eggs, 40
Stir-frying: general rules, 37
Sukiyaki-style beef, 100
Swordfish: fragrant
swordfish with ginger
and lemongrass, 66
Szechuan eggplant, 129

T

Teriyaki sauce, 14
Thai fish cakes: fried
Singapore noodles, 175
Thai fish stir-fry, 72
Thai-fried vegetables in
wonton cups, 49
Thai green curry
paste, 22
Thai red curry paste, 22

Thai salsa: spicy vegetable
fritters with Thai
salsa, 136
Tofu: red-cooked tofu
with Chinese
mushrooms, 142
stir-fried tofu and
beansprouts with
noodles, 178
Turkey: stir-fried
turkey with broccoli
and shiitake
mushrooms, 104
turkey with sage, prunes
and brandy, 118
Turmeric, 12

V

Veal escalopes with
artichokes, 85
Vegetables: crispy
noodles with mixed
vegetables, 158
deep-fried root
vegetables with
spiced salt, 133
marinated mixed
vegetables with
basil oil, 139
mixed roasted
vegetables, 144

oriental vegetable
noodles, 169
spiced vegetables
with coconut, 130
spicy vegetable
fritters with Thai
salsa, 136
stir-fried vegetables with
coriander omelet, 126
stir-fried vegetables
with pasta, 183
Thai-fried vegetables in
wonton cups, 49
vegetable fajita, 157
vegetable tempura, 42
Vermicelli: mee krob, 167

W

Water chestnuts: steamed
spiced pork and water
chestnut wontons, 38
Wine vinegar, 14
Wok, 8

Y

Yellow flower vegetables, 134